# Dedication;

## To

— My wife, Jay, for supporting and believing in me
since the day we met.

— Our parents, Julia MacDonald and Howard and Eva Nixon,
for always being there.

— My children, Mitch, Geoff, and Stephanie,

— My brother, Robert (Baker) MacDonald

# **A**cknowledgements

What started out as a day of typing down ideas has lead to the publication of this book. It was, however, the support, the ability to provide feedback, and the editing skills of my wife, Jay, throughout the journey that has really made the difference. Thanks to Kelly Lovering whose enthusiasm for my project was a spark for my own renewed enthusiasm. Thanks to Don McKee, Coaching Committee Chairman, CHA, and Jamie McDonald, Director of Development, CHA, for their support and efforts toward this project.

I'd also like to thank photographers Roy Antel and Bryan Scholosser for their work; Boyd Kane for posing for the front cover; the hockey players and the Selinger family who participated in the photographs; Play It Again Sports in Regina for providing equipment for the photo shoots; and Rollie Bourassa for providing his talents toward a large number of the illustrations.

To all of my coaches, especially Ted Lewis and Gil Bernardin, a special thank you for volunteering their time and giving encouragement to me when I was a young player.

# About the Author

Leo MacDonald has developed a wealth of coaching expertise through experiences in junior and university coaching positions. The owner and director of a hockey school, he has worked with hockey players of all ages using many of the scrimmages and drills in this book. He is an ongoing student of the game, looking for ways of improving the success rates of players and teams. As he completes his coaching certification, achieving Master Coach status with the Canadian Hockey Association, Leo brings with him the development of new materials and methods.

As a coach, Leo maintains sound on-ice and off-ice principles backed by his understanding of the game and his desire to be aware of new research and innovative ideas. It is with this frame of mind that he has written this book.

Leo's educational background brings a scientific and theory-based approach to his book, *Perfect Practice*. His ability to clearly illustrate the premise of game-specific coaching results in an easy-to-follow text for coaches at all levels.

# Table of Contents

## SECTION FOUR – OFF-ICE TRANSFER TRAINING

*Street hockey has been a favorite of all ages for generations.*

# Preface

As a youngster I loved to play sports. Growing up with 50 kids on my block, there were always plenty of friends around to organize a game of some kind. Street hockey, football, baseball, whatever we wanted to do, we did it. Come winter, we'd hit the outdoor rink. And when we'd get together on the rink, we played shinny. Why shinny? Simply because it was fun.

Without knowing it we were greatly improving our skills and game sense because of the play. It is because of this point that coaches should recognize the merits of play. Most hockey practices are drills sequenced over the course of the allotted practice time. Including scrimmages is a positive aspect of practicing.

Have they worked on their skills? Yes. Have they had fun? Absolutely. Will it be transferable to actual game play? Definitely.

My son has always impressed me with his hockey sense. Having only reached Atom, he has a head for the game that is above his skills. It has occurred to me through my research reading that it is because of the experience he has gained beyond his years. Since the time he was three months old he has been at 25 to 30 junior hockey games a year, with his mom, watching the teams I have coached. By the time he was three or four years old, seeing those players on the ice began to have some meaning. He started to process what he was seeing. At home he had an old hockey game set from which we had removed the rods. He would play for hours with the players, moving them around, passing the puck, copying what he had seen the night before when he cheered on his favorite team.

The hockey set is long gone but the knowledge it gave him through play has carried over to his own game. This aptitude for the game can be taught and so should become an important objective of practice.

Today, as a hockey coach and teacher I've been seeking and discovering new ideas toward the development of athletic potential. The methods and drills in this book are provided to improve the learning potential and, consequently, performance.

# Introduction

How often has a skill or pattern of play been practiced but not executed during a game? One reason may be that the drills being used are not effective in the transference of skills and concepts. Game-like conditions have not been imposed and the result is non-execution during games.

It is the improved use of training time that is the key to potentially improving the quality of your athletes. This book provides methods for improving time usage, programs, drills, and games that you may use, and even modify, toward the development of your players. Practice sessions should be diverse and have a purpose, to produce results. The objective is to improve the quality and mechanics of practice sessions and to reach the ultimate – the perfect practice!

*"Practice doesn't make perfect, perfect practice makes perfect."*

# SECTION ONE

# Foundations for Coaching

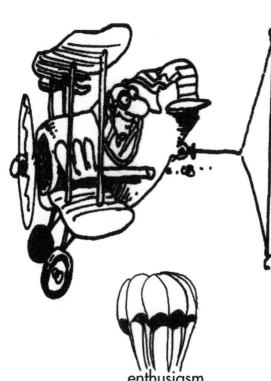

Communication

"Growth & Development"

enthusiasm

dedication

discipline

positive reinforcement

Coaching Foundations

# CHAPTER 1

## Communication

*"The key to successful coaching is through effective communication."*

Communication is the primary tool in shaping and preparing both the athlete and the team for competition. Weak communication skills will contribute to poor playing environments and performance breakdowns, and as such, communication must be a strong attribute if any coach is to be successful. No matter what the age of the athlete, positive and enjoyable playing environments allow for and actually promote enhanced performances. Under such conditions motivation and enthusiasm have the opportunity to "step forward" and become the characteristic or identity of the athlete, and ultimately the team.

Positive reinforcement is the method that is used the most often by successful coaches. It is a method that brings about a focus of success, confidence, and self-esteem to the competing athlete. Positive reinforcement, in which performance or behavior is accentuated by praise, is a form of communication that has a place in all levels of play. Young athletes in the minor hockey levels are developing new skills and experiencing new situations during the course of play. Overlearning these new skills and experiencing measures of success in situations of play only comes about through positive reassurance from the coach. The motivation to learn and to succeed are enhanced by the supportive nature of the coach. The coach who continually belittles or ignores effort corrodes the athlete's confidence and self-esteem. The timeline toward overlearning skills is extended and the athlete's attitude – and ultimately the team's – toward play is diminished.

Positive reinforcement must fall within the team structure of expectations. Expectations of behavior and effort are to be well defined by the coach and accepted by the players. Being positive without being firm, toward those defined expectations, leaves the possible perception of the coach being too soft. Such a perception can lead to a weakened playing environment and a less than satisfactory effort toward play. Positive reinforcement and discipline can and should coexist.

The coach who is enthusiastic and enjoys the opportunity to work with players without heed of personal gain is the coach who most likely will promote the positive environment. Enthusiasm and communication skills are the trademarks of successful coaching.

# CHAPTER 2

## Growth and Development

*"Recognizing the differences between the phases of growth and development is the first step toward successful coaching."*

At what ages do we implement our programs for physical and conceptual development? The National Coaching Certification Program identifies the Preadolescence Phase as being up to 11 years of age. It is this phase where technical foundations are being built. It is also the phase that is of particular importance to speed development. The Preadolescent's nervous system is particularly receptive to outside stimulus.

Dramatic improvements in muscular speed can be achieved by encouraging all-out efforts or through the intention of speed at this phase of development.

Going through drills as fast as possible without diminishing proper form or playing any other activity or game with the intention of being fast will stimulate that young nervous system. Training the nervous system in such a way will increase speed, allowing the individual to move closer toward genetic potential. "If you want to be fast, then go fast" is a simple and direct phrase that is understood by Preadolescents and encourages them toward increased speed.

This is not without recognizing the need for technical development. Teaching and practicing proper technique is very important, and is arguably the precursor to imposing speed demands. Realistically however, coaches do not have enough practice time to devote entirely to technical development. The player must spend his own time toward the refinement and reinforcement of skills. Coaches should, however, emphasize proper technique during the course of practice so as to fully take advantage of the concept of speed improvement.

The concept of **intention of speed** is not limited to the Preadolescent Phase. Although the nervous system is extremely receptive at the Preadolescent Phase it is also trainable throughout all the phases of growth and development.

Conceptually training the young athlete is equally, if not more, important and is something that should not be done without clear objectives. Preadolescent athletes and Early Adolescent athletes (11-13 year olds) need to be taught the general concepts of the game. Recognition of patterns or situations of play such as the give and go or angle checking are concepts that are pivotal in understanding the game. Often concepts are taught in a line drill or a chalk board setting, yet seldom pointed out and reinforced within an actual game simulation. It is game simulation that is the final phase in transference of concepts and skills.

During these two age phases the young athlete is particularly receptive to conceptual learning. Youngsters are not given enough credit for what their learning capabilities really are. Motivated athletes at these particular phases are akin to little sponges – absorbing information and eagerly applying what they have learned at every opportunity. It becomes important then as a coach to teach the concepts in a way that is appropriate for the age level.

Transition as a concept, for example, is taught at the Preadolescent Phase through headmanning drills and is reinforced using game simulations or scrimmages. The desired outcome here is quick puck movement to gain ice quickly. In other words, we are looking to move the puck up to a single player without being overly concerned about the movement of the rest.

As the athletes' skills improve with age, the concept of transition is broadened. It is broadened to include patterns of play that involve groups of players attempting to gain ice in numbers. Now the focus is on the movement of the whole group of players; where each should be in relation to the puck, and its various destinations. As such, new concepts are applied and intermeshed. The single concept of headmanning has included several concepts, such as timing and support, so that a successful counter or regroup is attainable by the players; it is no longer just about headmanning the puck quickly. Thus, by identifying the objective (e.g., transition) one can ascertain the appropriate outcome (e.g., headmanning or group counter attacks) by what the players are capable of handling and apply the concepts accordingly.

*"As a coach, the difficult part is not applying concepts to the appropriate levels, it is determining the appropriate outcome."*

Recognizing the differences between the phases of growth and development is important. It allows for the proper coaching of young players, resulting in not only happier players but more gratifying experiences for the coaches as well. Young athletes should be encouraged and supported to participate in activities outside the game of hockey itself. This will enhance greatly the social, mental, and emotional as well as the physical development of the young athletes, leading to healthier and happier personalities. The result will be stronger, more motivated players with the associated characteristics required to play hockey at the elite levels to which young players throughout the world aspire.

# SECTION TWO

# Transfer
# Training

**Transfer Training is "driven" by specificity and athleticism.**

# CHAPTER 3

## Physical Performance Factors

*"The concepts of specificity and athleticism are the 'vehicles' that allow the athlete to reach the objective of quality training and accelerated learning."*

The maximization of time and the improved transference from practice to actual performance are the objectives of any coach when training teams. By improving the quality of practice, game performance will improve. This applies not only to on-ice sessions but to off-ice sessions as well.

Transfer Training is a method that embodies the idea of transference in learning. It is this transference in learning, from practice to game, that is the goal. By improving the quality of game simulation within practice sessions or introducing game simulation within conditioning programs, the rate of transference to game performance is accelerated. As a result, the quality of training has improved. Transfer Training looks to facilitate the transfer of two main aspects – physical skills and conceptual skills.

## Physical Skills

The transfer of physical skills from practice to game play is engineered by using methods that adhere to the concepts of **specificity** and **athleticism.**

Specificity is defined as movements that reflect or simulate the actual movements used during the performance of the chosen sport. Athleticism refers to the individual's qualities of agility, balance, speed, coordination, strength, power, flexibility, and endurance. The idea of athleticism plays a prominent role in the speed and quality of transference an athlete may potentially attain.

The concepts of specificity and athleticism are the "vehicles" that allow the athlete to reach the objective of quality training and accelerated learning.

## Specificity

If the goal is to become a better hockey player, hockey specific skills and awareness must be rehearsed as much as possible. Recognizing that leads to the question of "How?" The answer is through the concept of specificity in training. This allows for practice and training to become more transferable to the actual outcome – improved game performance.

It is specificity that conditions the player. It conditions in such a way as to allow for easier replication and performance of a desired skill or decision during actual competition. An example would be to use drills that directly mimic situations as they may occur during the course of an actual game. A shooting drill in which the shooter is under pressure intensifies not only the decision-making process but the physical demands as well. As a result the athlete is placed into a game-like situation.

Controlled scrimmages, in which desired movements or decisions are pointed out, are another example. As such, training time has become more specific and time usage maximized. There are many examples in which mimicking a movement produces a positive transference effect.

*"Most importantly, it is clear that the more specific or closely related a movement is to the actual movement desired, the greater the rate of transference."*

# Athleticism

Athleticism is important in fully developing athletic ability. **An athlete with a higher level of athleticism will learn skills faster, and will react or respond to the challenges of game play faster, than an athlete who has a low level of athleticism.** Cross training (being involved in different activities such as golf, baseball, soccer) is a popular method of "training" that is very beneficial to younger players in particular. By exposing the individual to other sports and sport settings, athleticism is improved through the rehearsing of new movement patterns, using

*Being involved in different activities improves the rate of an athlete's development, physically and mentally.*

different instruments of play. This exposure leads to the complete development of athleticism and lets the athlete enjoy the variety of activities available while breaking the monotony of single sport training.

Athleticism can be improved during practices by varying the space available to play in, varying the difficulty of the task, utilizing unusual starting positions, altering the speed or rhythm of performance, and varying the rules to meet your objectives of play. For example, stickhandling variations may include: using various points on the stickblade; using one or two hands; from various positions such as the knees; under opponent pressure; a stickhandling-before-passing rule; or by varying the space (jumping/dodging obstacles for example).

Athleticism is further enhanced by applying the concept of **symmetrization** within a training program. By training the non-dominant side or limb, overall motor coordination is dramatically improved in a short period of time. Starosta (1988) postulated that this dramatic improvement is because training the "weaker" limb forces analytical thinking or imagery to mirror the performance. This consequently reinforces those elements associated with proper performance. The idea of practicing both physically and mentally is particularly important for young athletes.

An example is having a player practice stickhandling with the opposite hand and then returning to the preferred hand. Symmetrization is also accomplished by emphasizing a switch in starting direction for drills so that both sides of the body are worked. Using methods such as these within a practice will increase athleticism and thereby enhance skill level.

# Chapter 4

## Conceptual Performance – "A.K.A." Decision Making

*"Decision making is the foundation that determines the level of success achieved by athletes."*

The end result of several conceptual factors, including experience and abstract thinking, decision making is the cornerstone of game sense. It allows the athlete to further comprehend the game of hockey, and to recognize the ever changing environment with the objective of responding as quickly and accurately as possible. A perfect example is hockey's Great One. Wayne Gretzky reads the play so well that he has shattered old standards and reestablished new standards of offensive ability over the course of his extraordinary career. He has done so with a high skill level, governed by a brilliant hockey mind.

Teaching players to think in practice sessions, and to improve the success rate of decisions made during the course of practice, will improve performance during competition. The smart hockey player is able to elevate his play and his potential. While skills are very important to successful performance, it is the athlete's conceptual abilities that make the difference. A common analogy used by hockey scouts of "having the tools, but no toolbox," is in reference to the athlete's lack of game sense.

ALL THE TOOLS...BUT... NO TOOLBOX!

With examples such as Gretzky, an emphasis toward **conceptual training should be an objective of all coaches when planning training sessions.** However, this is arguably not the case at present. Practices have tended to be skill orientated, with little emphasis toward the thinking part of the game. To rectify this, coaches have to look at identifying concepts, simulating concepts, and rehearsing concepts during training sessions.

# Experience

Experience is the recognition of an event or situation and the predictability of the outcome. For example, a player knows that by passing the puck off the boards at a certain angle the result will be redirection out at the same angle. This experience is developed not only by actually performing the event but also by observing the event. **It is observation and performance that develop experience** but experience alone is not enough to improve decision making. Using the boards to pass the puck past a defender to open ice does not mean that the play has been read or perceived correctly. Experience is not the equivalent of abstract thinking. It does allow for a structure or set of "rules" to follow so that results are predictable. We know that if we do something, such as a bounce pass off the boards, the resulting puck movement is predictable. Because it does not take into account player interaction, experience is limited on its own. However, in concert with other performance factors, such as abstract thinking, successful team play is the result.

# Abstract Thinking

The ability to understand situations without having to see the actual people or objects involved and to anticipate or "think ahead" toward predicting probable outcomes is abstract thinking. In the game of chess, for example, players must think abstractly to plan advantageous moves without actually touching the pieces. Once a move or series of moves is decided upon, the actual "first" move is physically taken.

In the dynamic sport of hockey, players read situations as they unfold and recognize possible solutions or outcomes. This recognition allows the player to react or make a decision based upon what he has recognized the situation to be. Recognition evolves from experience and familiarity. **It is experience and familiarity that improve a player's ability to think abstractly in relation to the game.**

Someone who has never played the game before would have trouble following a chalktalk. The experienced player, on the other hand, can visualize the concepts being taught. Players that play or scrimmage often see similar situations, develop over and over. Through trial and error or observing successful solutions, these players develop the abstract thinking that allows them to react successfully to the situations they experience. This concept is not restricted to certain stages of growth and development. A young child of nine years of age, for example, can develop and apply abstract thinking to the game of hockey. This is possible if the young player has enough experience and familiarity with the game through actual playing and observation. Nine year olds can have years of experience and familiarity, since in Canada it is not unusual to begin observing and playing the game at age three.

Abstract thinking will have its limitations according to the level of experience and methods of presentation. The coaches who use the Xs and Os on a chalkboard will not reach, cognitively speaking, those with poor abstract thinking. Those players will not be able to visualize and apply what has been drawn out as effectively as players with better developed abstract thinking. Even the young experienced player will have difficulty with the chalkboard. Pucks on the floor for example, since they are three dimensional, will provide better results in teaching young players.

# Chapter 5

## Performance Factors – An Application

*"Practice sessions must be designed to place the athlete
in game-like or specific simulations."*

Hockey is a dynamic sport. Situations are constantly changing during the course of a game, and players must react to this ever-changing environment. Physically and conceptually speaking, specificity is achieved and decision making is practiced with drills and scrimmages that are game-like in nature.

By placing the player in game-like drills during practice, the transfer of rehearsed characteristics to the actual game itself is more likely to be achieved. With this in mind one can see that, by playing out a drill to its possible outcomes, the player is maintaining his focus on the task at hand and working toward a complete objective. In contrast, traditional drills are not played out and, therefore, the objectives are only partly achieved or not at all.

An example is the traditional Two-on-One drill. Usually the drill concludes with a shot on goal or the defender denying the attackers a shot. The puck ends up sliding off in one direction and the combatants casually skate back to their respective spots in line, to wait for their next turn. By emphasizing game specificity, the drill takes on a new look. Now the Two-on-One is not complete until the defender successfully contains the attackers and clears the puck to an awaiting outlet player; the goalie freezes the puck; or the attackers score a goal. Practicing in this manner fulfills game simulation objectives completely and improves the transition from practice to actual game performance. This transference is our prime objective. The Link Concept, discussed in Chapter 7, is an example of Transfer Training.

How often have we heard of the great players who spent countless hours playing shinny with their buddies? This is where they learned to recognize situations and honed their skills. The ability to read the situation and react creatively is the skill that produces the players of legendary status; the Beliveaus, Gretzkys, and Lemieuxs. Replicating this learning can be accomplished through the use of scrimmages and drills that maximize the transference potential.

> *"It was the ponds where skills were developed – scrimmages recreate the pond."*
>
> **Kelly Lovering, Former Chair, CHA Coaching Committee**

When scrimmaging, all facets of the game come into play, allowing for repeated rehearsal of not only the skill aspects, but most certainly the conceptual part of hockey. Specialized scrimmages place the player into game-like situations with the coach setting out certain objectives to be practiced. Those objectives may be, for example, the skills of saucer passing and puck control, where the game is played with one type of pass only (saucer). The player must now react to the simulated conditions of the specialized scrimmage while keeping the objectives of the drill in mind. This type of scrimmaging encompasses both conceptual and skill development, the two most important facets of being a complete hockey player.

Practices can be planned to involve purposeful scrimmage play. The result is that ice usage is maximized, a level of fun is injected, and the conceptual components of hockey are rehearsed, allowing for an easier transition to actual performance.

Anatoli Tarasov (1969), the great Russian coach, felt that game-like conditions played an important role in planning effective practices.

# SECTION THREE

# On-Ice Transfer Training

*Scrimmaging can take various forms.*
*Inside-Out Hockey (above) gives*
*players a different perspective.*

# CHAPTER 6

## Specialized Scrimmage

*"Scrimmages must have a purpose – an objective."*

Over the past decade, the use of scrimmages as a form of technical and tactical development has been drastically reduced within the coach's practice plan. The cost and availability of facilities have magnified the importance of maximum use of practice time, yet the usage of game simulation drills such as scrimmages has declined. The understanding and the use of game simulation play in its various forms will allow for the simultaneous development of the athlete's technical and tactical skills.

As with any practice method, scrimmages must have a purpose – an objective. By doing so, specialized scrimmages will be a more accepted method of practice. By combining specific objectives within play, both skill and conceptual attributes may improve at a quicker rate. Transference from practice to actual performance will be achieved with greater success with a well-planned practice that includes specialized scrimmage drills.

The idea of game-centered teaching, as a form of conceptual and skill development is a reflection of the individual's motivation to play. All athletes, young and old, want to play and as such are highly motivated when introduced to game play (specialized scrimmage) as a form of practice. Using game simulation techniques, and introducing and emphasizing objectives during play, develops the conceptual components of experience and abstract thinking. Players learn to think during the course of play. They learn to recognize situations, decide a course of action, and execute a play. It is this read and react development that so often does not receive the attention it should, and because of this, development is usually left to those countless shinny games on rinks and streets around the country.

Skill development is also a requirement that can be an objective of game simulation play. Knowing that players are motivated to play, skill improvements as a training objective can be incorporated within specialized scrimmages. Specialized scrimmage is a method that allows the athlete to develop both skill and conceptual aspects. For example, a Three-on-Three scrimmage where the players must pass to an outlet (usually the coach) and drive the net for a return pass. All the skills are being rehearsed, but the concept of driving and support is emphasized.

**Practices should involve a blend or mix of drills and simulations for maximum athletic development.** Introducing specialized scrimmage to young athletes throughout the course of a training cycle is important. It's fun, and the motivation toward improvement increases. The incorporation of specialized scrimmage has its place with older athletes as well.

By using specialized scrimmages that emphasize certain skills, both the necessary techniques and decision making are practiced. The small country of Finland has made great inroads in the development of their young hockey players. With a lack of facilities coupled with a great demand, hockey coaches in Finland have devised a series of small group games that allow for maximum usage of ice time which, in turn, speeds up the development process. The use of these small group games within practice sessions allows for a greater degree of skill rehearsal and the subsequent recognition of situations as they occur. Game sense is developed with these drills, along with the physical skills necessary for participation.

*"It is only by playing that a player truly develops an understanding of the game."*

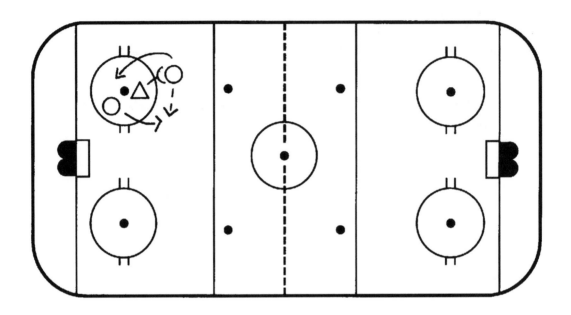

# Give-and-Go Game

Three players or more are used. In a small area two players maintain puck control away from the lone pursuer. The pass receiver may only take two strides to ensure the passer moves to an opening for a return pass. The player giving away the puck becomes "it" (pursuer).

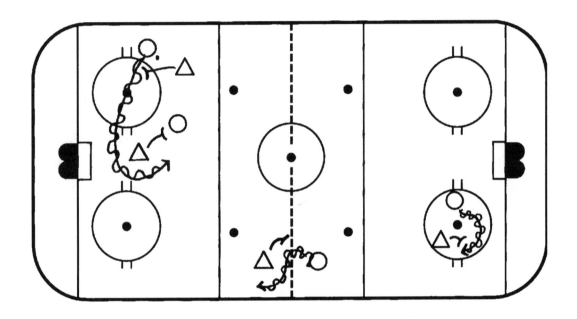

# Keepaway

Using a one-on-one or small group situation, players play in one zone or a designated area such as the circles. The objective is to keep the puck away from your opponents.

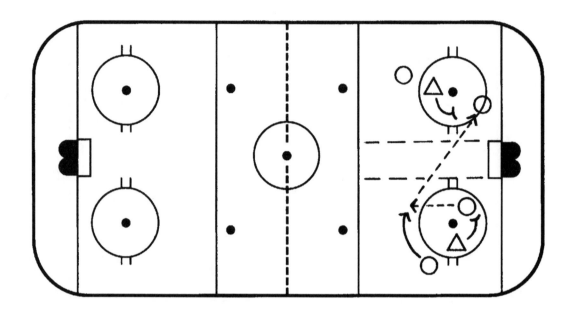

# Twilight Zone

This is a variation of the Give-and-Go game. Six players are needed, two pursuers and four controllers. Pylons are placed to indicate the area where no player may enter. Passes may be made across this area to awaiting teammates. Angling, anticipation, and area containment are practiced by the pursuers.

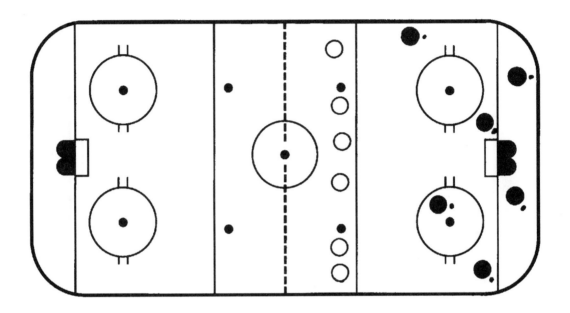

# Team Keepaway

Two teams of any size are used. One team has pucks in a designated area (usually a zone). On a whistle, the team without the pucks enters the zone, attempting to clear all the pucks out of the zone. When the last puck clears the zone, the teams exchange roles. The objectives are one-on-one puck control and support concepts. The team maintaining puck control the longest wins. The focus could shift to the team clearing the pucks the fastest being the winner.

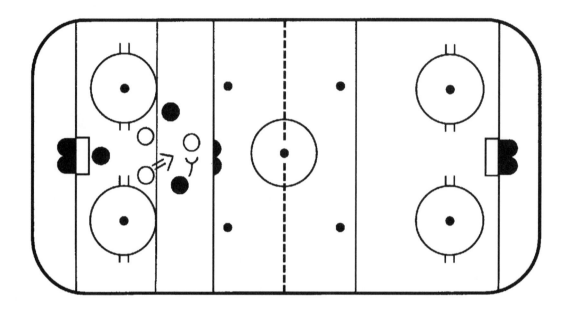

# Wrist Shot Game

Two teams of three are needed. Each team has two shooters and one attacker. The two shooters must stay on their half of the space to shoot and play defense against the opposing attacker. The attacker roams the offensive space only or parks in front of the net. The attacker is active, looking to score while the defenders (shooters) contain, control, and then shoot the puck, looking to initiate their own offense. No players may cross over the half in which they play.

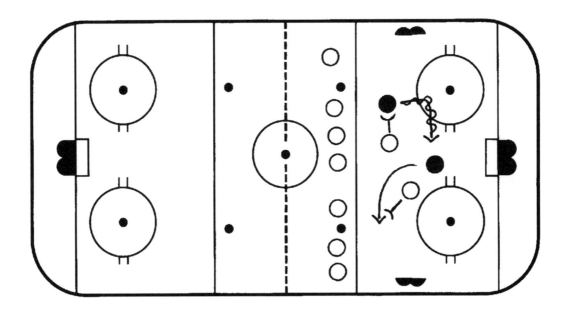

# Two-On-Two Game

This is a small area scrimmage that simulates all aspects of play. This game can be modified to one-on-one or three-on-three. Use short, intense shifts of thirty seconds. If a goal is scored before the end of a shift, throw another puck out for the scrimmage to continue.

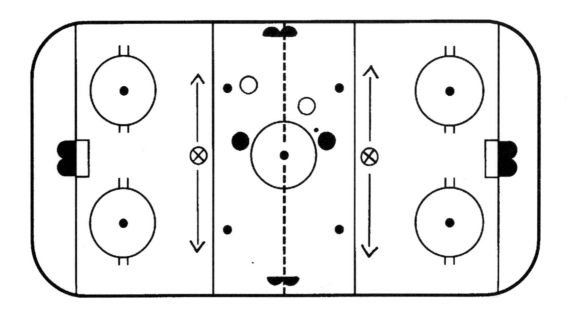

# Sliding Wingers

A small area game with two teams of two scrimmaging. The Sliding Wingers are neutral and stay on the outside boundaries. The game is a continuous odd-man situation. The Sliding Wingers are allowed to shoot.

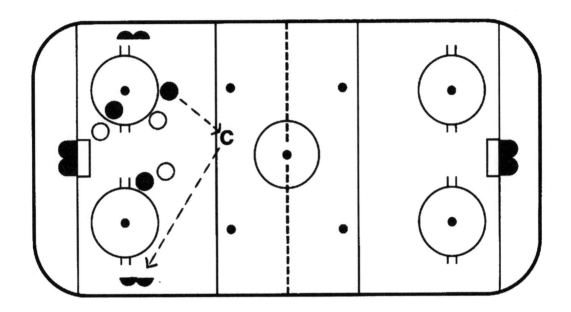

# Three-on-Three Outlet

A small area game that has the coach at the outside midpoint spot. The teams must pass to the coach to initiate an offensive attack. The coach can pass to a player or shoot at the net. Driving the net, regroups, and breakouts are among the objectives to be practiced.

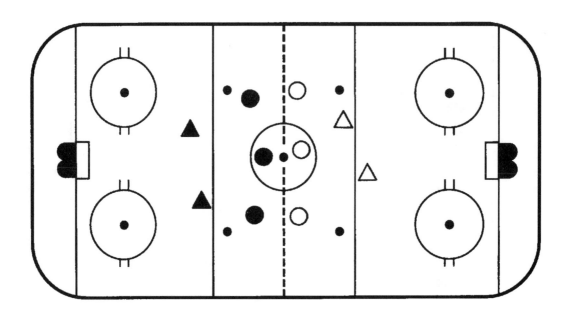

# Opposite Hands

A scrimmage game that is played using the nonpreferred hand. This game may be played on full ice or in designated areas with appropriate numbers.

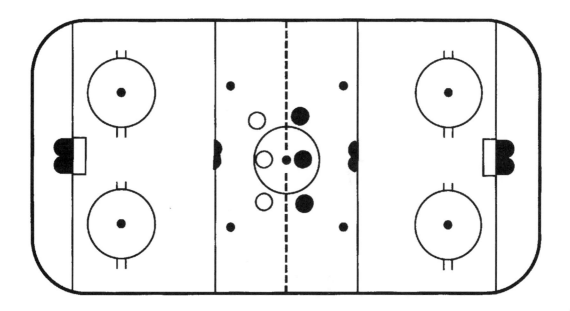

# Inside-Out Hockey

Two teams of three or four are used. The nets are moved up to the blue lines and turned facing the end boards. Face-offs are used as normal. Scrimmaging in this way emphasizes back-of-the-net play and an overall different "look".

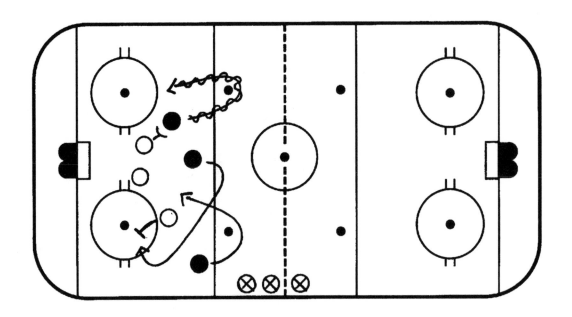

# Replay

Three teams of three are needed. A game of three against three is played in one zone. The team that scores continues to play. To be on offense the puck must be cleared out and brought back in. This is a competitive conditioning game.

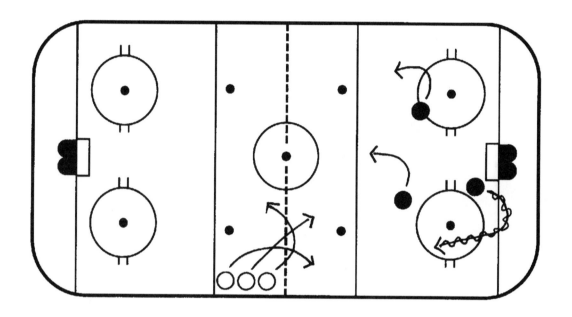

# Continuous

A three-on-three or four-on-four game played on full ice. The team that scores retrieves the puck and attacks the end from which they came. A new defensive team rushes on while the team scored upon hustles off the ice.

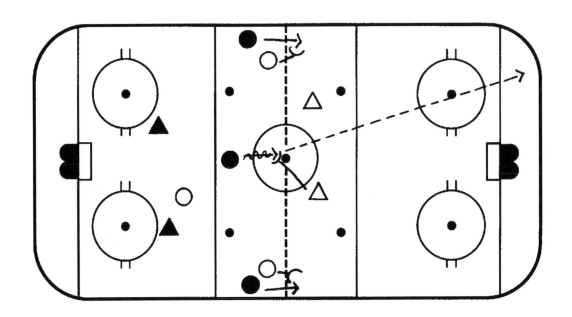

# Dump and Chase Game

A scrimmage in which the puck may not be carried into the offensive zone. The puck must be dumped in. Forechecking and coverage are continually practiced with this game.

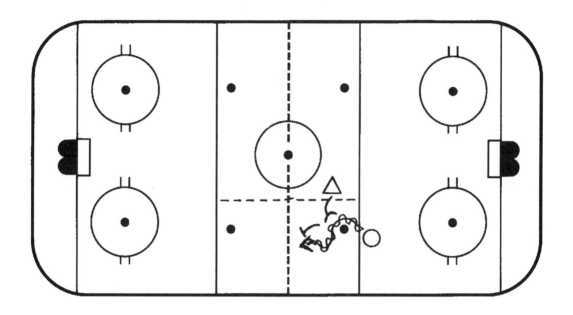

# Contain Game

This is played one-on-one in a small area. On command, the offensive player attacks, trying to cross the far line. The defender steps up and plays to "contain" not check, the attacking player. The offensive player has ten seconds to move across the space to the other side.

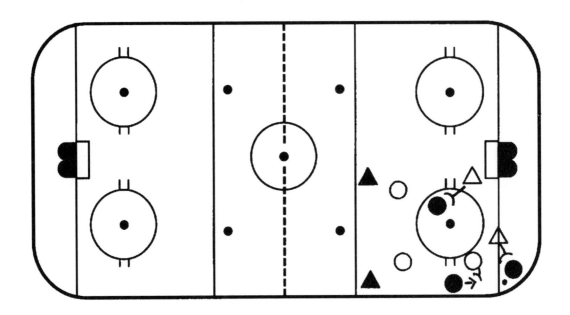

# D Zone Game

Teams of three to five are used. The attacking team has two min-utes to score as often as possible. During this time the defenders try to break out or clear the puck out of the zone. If they are suc-cessful, another puck is immediately fed into the zone. When time is up, the teams switch roles. The team scoring the most wins.

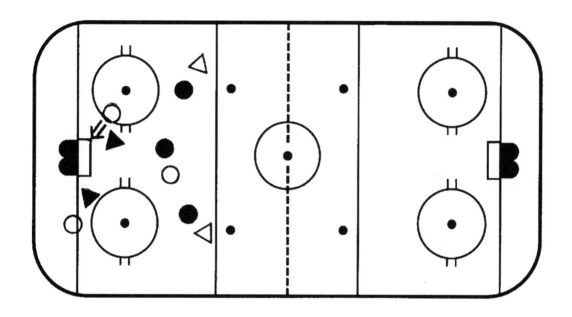

# The Go-Ahead Game

Two teams of five scrimmage. When a goal is scored, the net into which the goal is scored on becomes "unscorable". The team that was scored on, must score before a predetermined period of time (e.g., two minutes) has elapsed. If they are successful, the game starts over. If they are unsuccessful, the team preventing the tying goal earns one point and a new game begins.

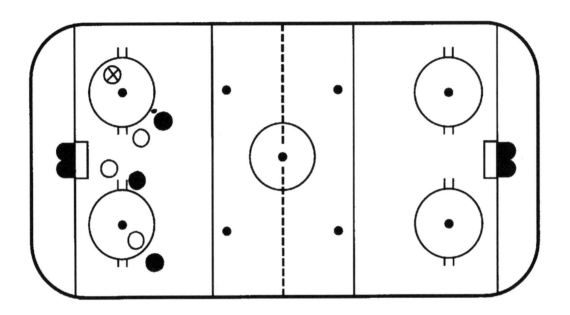

# The Rover

This may be played as a small area or full-ice game. Two teams of equal number play against one another. An extra player (rover) in a distinct color also plays. The rover plays for whichever team has possession of the puck. This creates continuous odd-man situations. Play continues to a predetermined number of goals (e.g., 3 goals)

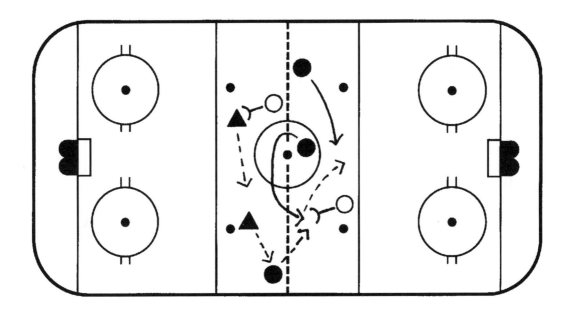

# Ping Pong

This is a five-on-two small ice game. The team of five must "one touch" pass or give up possession. The two-man team has no restrictions. The objective is to enhance puck movement.

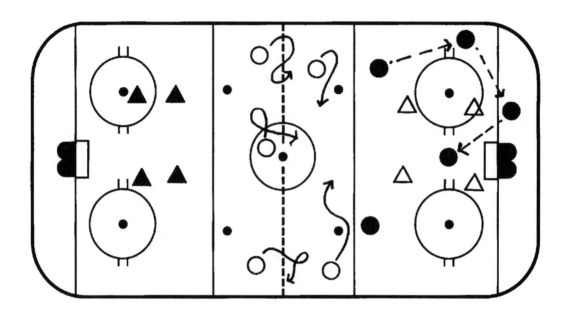

# Powerplay Game

Two teams of nine are needed with one powerplay unit and one penalty killing unit per team. As one team is on the powerplay, the defending team will have their powerplay unit at neutral ice waiting for the puck. When the defending team gains possession of the puck, it is passed up to their powerplay unit. Upon receiving the puck from the penalty killers, the powerplay unit then attacks the other team's penalty killing unit waiting in the far zone.

This game is continuous and can be modified to a five-on-three or a four-on-three situation

# Chapter 7

## The Linking Concept

*"By playing out a drill to its possible outcomes the player is maintaining his focus on the task at hand and working toward a complete objective."*

Making the most out of valuable practice time is the premise of Transfer Training. By improving the quality of the drills used, the quality of practice proportionately improves. An obvious observation is that the athlete's effort is tantamount to the success of any drill devised by the coaching staff. But, providing the best vehicle for quality practices will enable the athlete to accelerate his progress. The satisfaction of seeing improvement will increase his enthusiasm for practice.

In the game of hockey, the speed and ever-changing situations place demands on the athlete that require recognition, and the technical skills for adjustment and reaction. This means that training or practice sessions must be designed to place the athlete in game-like simulations. Rehearsing under game-like conditions strengthens the athlete's decision-making skills and shortens the transfer time of improved playing ability from practice to actual competition. Over the last decade, practices have taken on a line drill orientation that usually concludes with an unfinished play in the attacking zone. Because of this, coaches have lost an

Ever get the feeling something's missing?

opportunity to fully incorporate simulation within their drills. The shift in play from offense to defense or defense to offense is usually not completely incorporated (Westerlund, Personal Communication, 1994).

The traditional One-on-One is an example of a drill that can be linked with the concept of transitional play. By playing out the One-on-One and concluding the first sequence by either scoring a goal or moving the puck up to a waiting forward (defense to offense) the drill has achieved full game simulation. This addresses transitional play. A player must react defensively and offensively repeatedly over the course of a shift. Understanding when to react and how to react can be taught. This conceptual and physical reaction is practiced over and over by game-specific drills.

By incorporating the **Linking Concept**, game play is simulated. Simulation enables the athlete to practice precisely the objectives of the drill. The quality of practices will be improved and the transfer from practice sessions to competition will be enhanced.

*"It is the improved transfer from practice to competition that is the objective of both the coach and athlete."*

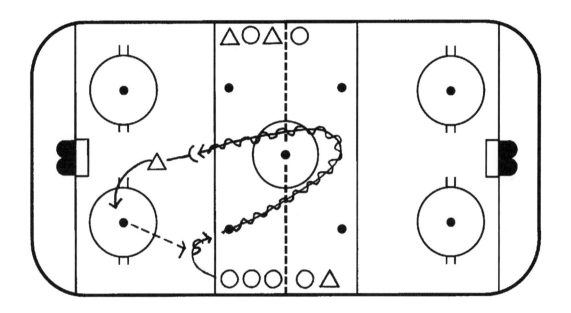

# One-on-One Link

A forward loops through neutral ice and plays one-on-one with a waiting defenseman. The one-on-one is played out until the puck is cleared, controlled by the goalie, or a goal is scored. During the play a supporting forward enters the zone. When the supporting forward gains control of the puck (loose or passed) he loops back through neutral ice to initiate a new one-on-one against a waiting defenseman.

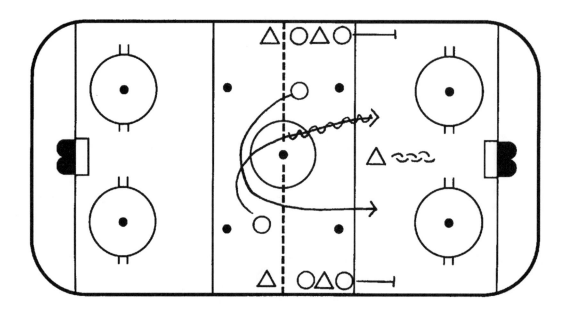

# Two-on-One Link

Two forwards loop through neutral ice and play a two-on-one against a defenseman. The situation is played out and supported by two new forwards who have entered the zone. The play is continued as the supporting forwards gain puck control and loop through neutral ice to initiate a new two-on-one against a waiting defenseman.

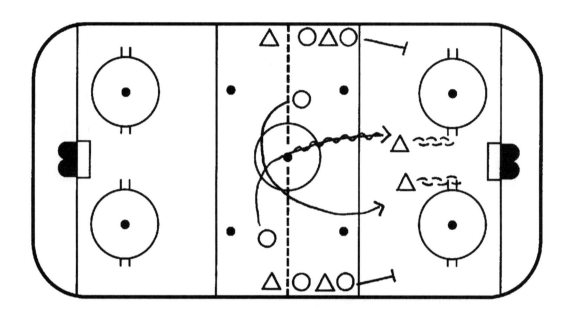

# Two-on-Two Link

Two forwards loop through neutral ice and play a two-on-two against the waiting defensemen. The situation is played out as two supporting forwards enter the zone. When the supporting forwards gain puck control, they loop through neutral ice to initiate a new two-on-two against the waiting defensemen.

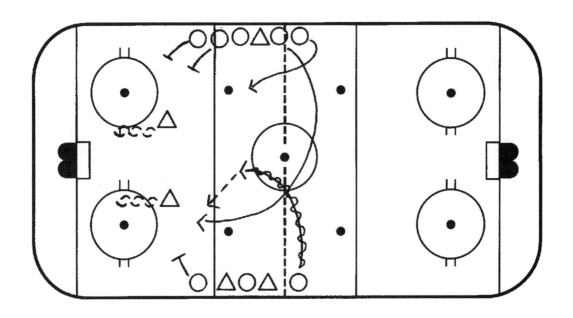

# Three-on-Two Link

Three forwards loop through neutral ice and play a three-on-two against the waiting defensemen. The situation is played out as three supporting forwards enter the zone. When the supporting forwards gain puck control, they initiate a new three-on-two against the waiting defensemen.

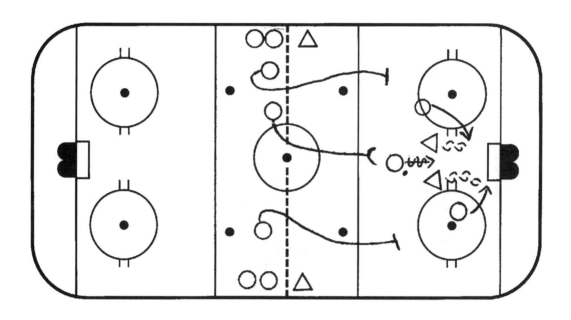

# Three-on-Two Full Ice

To start the drill three forwards curl into one zone and receive a pass from the goalie. These forwards rush up the ice against two waiting defensemen. As the rush enters the offensive zone, three supporting forwards join the play. The situation is played out. When the supporting forwards gain puck control, they rush up the ice against two new waiting defensemen creating a new three-on-two situation.

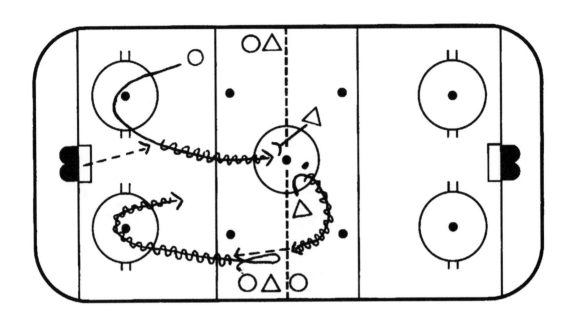

# One-on-Two Link

A forward loops through neutral ice and plays a one-on-two against the waiting defensemen. The play continues as a supporting forward enters the zone. The situation is played out and upon gaining puck control, the defensemen headman the puck to the supporting forward. This supporting forward curls deep into the defensive zone and initiates a new one-on-two.

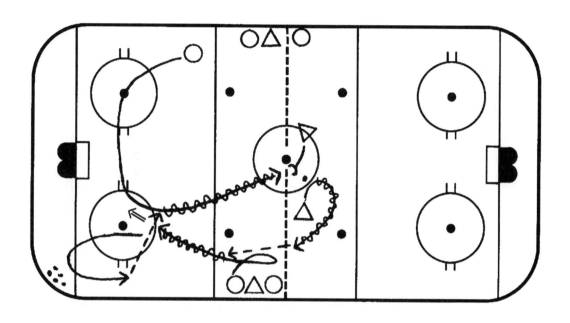

# One-on-Two Link (variation)

A forward loops through neutral ice and plays a one-on-two against the waiting defensemen. The play continues as a supporting forward enters the zone. The situation is played out and upon gaining puck control the defensemen headman the puck to the supporting forward. The supporting forward drives offensively and takes a shot on the net. After shooting, the forward swings into a corner, picks up a puck, and passes to a new curling forward. This curling forward initiates a new one-on-two.

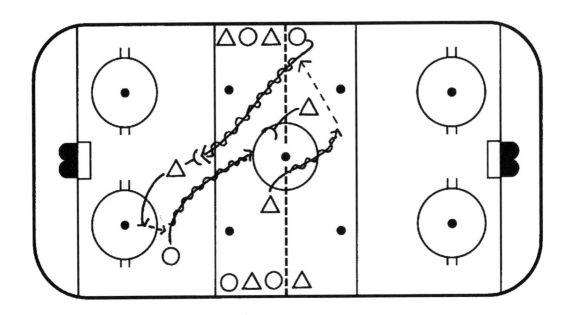

# Transition Link

This drill starts with a One-on-One Link and progresses to a one-on-two neutral ice situation. The breaking forward is met early (before the red line) by two defensemen who try to gain puck control. After checking the breaking forward, the defense headmans the puck to another forward skating through neutral ice. This forward then initiates a new one-on-one against a waiting defenseman.

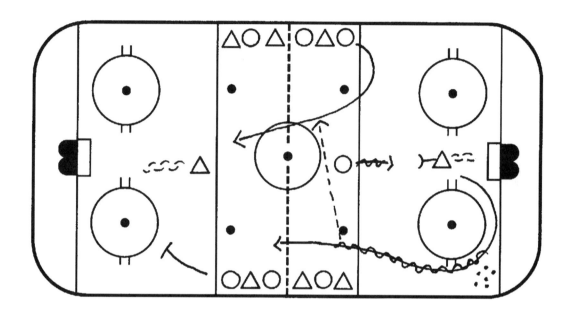

# Jumping Up

A one-on-one rush is initiated by a goalie pass to a curling forward. After the rush is broken up the defenseman passes the puck up to a supporting forward and joins the attack, creating a two-on-one rush. After the initial rush, the defenseman pulls out of the play leaving the possible one-on-one to play out. The defending defenseman looks to gain the puck, passes it up to a new supporting forward, and joins the attack up the ice.

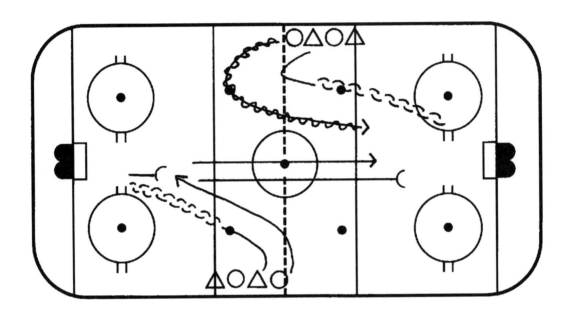

# One-on-One Transition

The drill is initiated with a one-on-one. On the whistle these one-on-one players race up the ice to join the new one-on-one initiated by that same whistle. The roles are switched as the defenseman jumps up to join the attack and the forward backchecks to support the defending defenseman. The situation is played out.

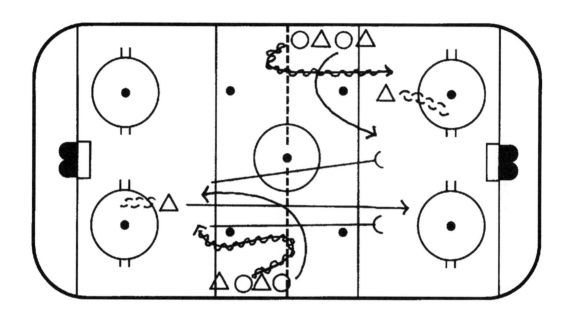

# Two-on-One Transition

The drill is initiated with a two-on-one. On the whistle these players race up the ice to join the new two-on-one initiated by that same whistle. The roles are switched as the defenseman joins the attack and the two forwards backcheck to support the lone defender. The situation is played out.

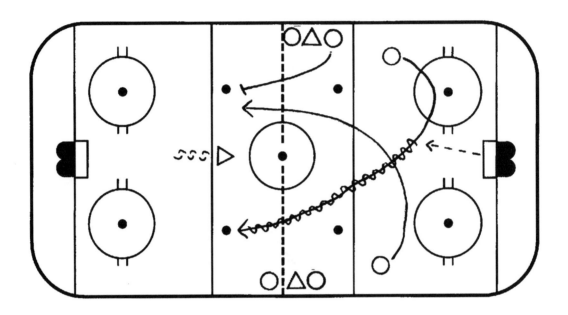

# Two-on-One Backcheck

The goalie initiates the drill by passing to one of two forwards curling deep in the defensive zone. These forwards rush up the ice two-on-one against a waiting defenseman. A backchecking forward joins the rush to assist the lone defenseman creating a two-on-two situation.

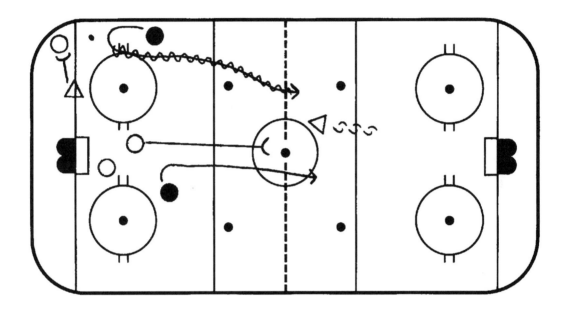

# Two-on-One Backcheck (continued)

As the situation is played out, two new supporting forwards enter the zone. Upon gaining puck control, the supporting forwards rush up the ice against a new waiting defenseman. The attacking forward from the original two-on-two that is highest in the zone backchecks to create the new two-on-two.

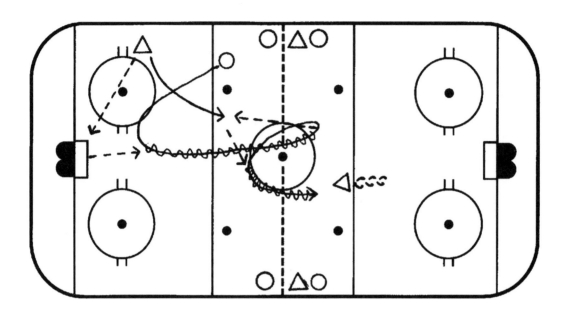

# One-on-One Regroup

A defenseman initiates the drill by passing to the goalie, who passes to the forward curling high in the defensive zone. The forward attacks one-on-one against a waiting defenseman. Upon crossing the red line, the forward turns back and regroups with the drill-initiating defenseman. After the regroup, the forward re-attacks one-on-one.

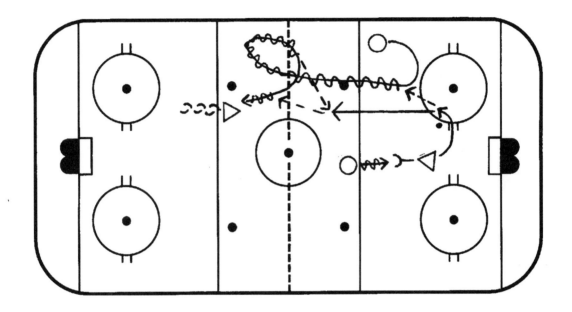

# One-on-One Regroup (continued)

As the situation is played out, a supporting forward enters the zone. Upon gaining puck control, the supporting forward rushes up the ice, creating a new one-on-one against a waiting defenseman.

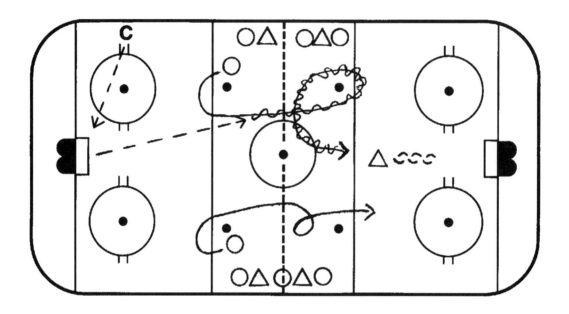

# Two-on-One Regroup

The coach initiates the drill by passing to the goalie, who passes to the forwards curling high in the defensive zone. The forwards rush down the ice two-on-one. As they hit the offensive blue line, the forwards turn back and regroup. After the regroup, the forwards continue two-on-one. The situation is played out and the defender is supported by two new forwards entering the zone.

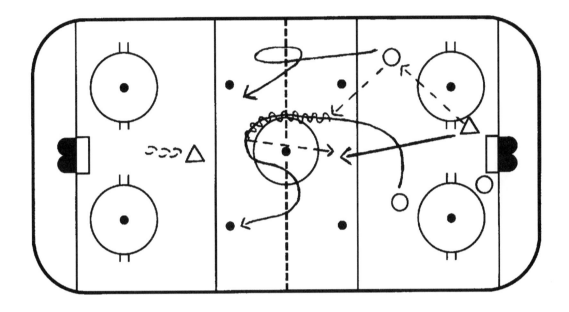

# Two-on-One Regroup (continued)

The play continues with a breakout by the supporting forwards. The forwards then regroup when they reach the offensive blue line. The breakout defenseman moves up the ice to participate in the regroup. After the regroup, the forwards attack two-on-one against a waiting defenseman.

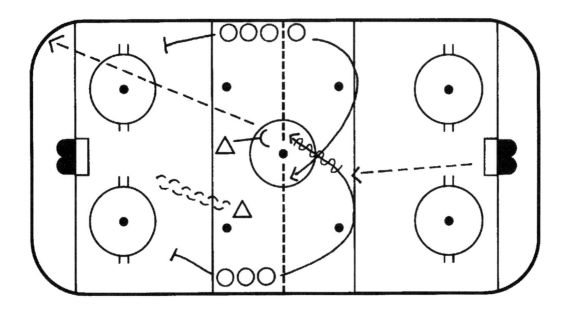

# Dump and Chase Twos

The goalie initiates the drill by passing to the forwards curling through the defensive zone. These two forwards attack two waiting defensemen and upon reaching the red line, they dump the puck into the offensive zone. As the forwards are forechecking, two supporting forwards enter the zone. The situation is played out and a new attack is initiated by the supporting forwards in the other direction.

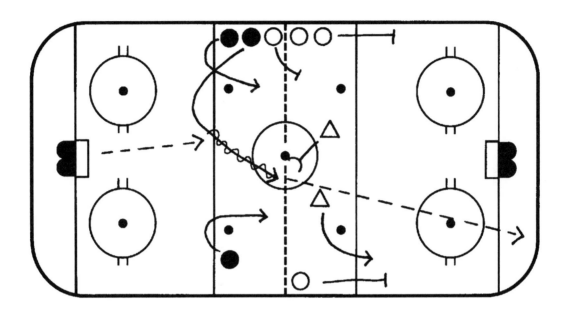

# Dump and Chase Threes

The goalie initiates the drill by passing to the forwards curling through the defensive zone. These three forwards attack two defensemen aided by a defending forward. Upon reaching the red line, the attacking forwards dump the puck into the offensive zone. As the attackers enter the zone, two supporting forwards enter to assist the defending forward already in the play. After the situation is played out, these three forwards would break out and attack in the other direction to continue the drill.

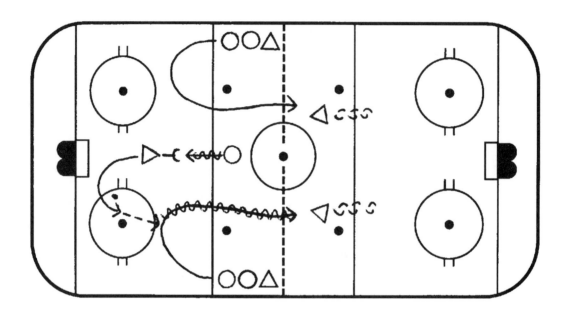

# Doubles (One-Two)

A continuous one-on-one, two-on-two drill. To start the drill a one-on-one is played out, and supported by two forwards. Upon gaining puck control, the supporting forwards rush up the ice two-on-two against two waiting defensemen. The situation is played out with a new supporting forward entering the zone looking to initiate a new one-on-one.

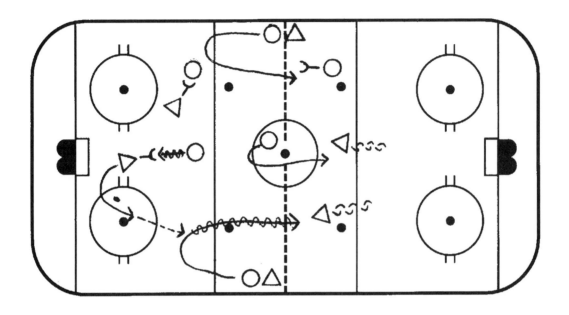

# Doubles (Two-Three)

The two-on-two, three-on-three doubles drill is a variation of the preceding drill. Begin with a two-on-two being played out. Three supporting forwards enter the zone. Upon gaining puck control, the supporting forwards rush up the ice against two waiting defensemen and a backchecking forward, creating a three-on-three. The situation is played out with two new supporting forwards entering the zone looking to initiate a new two-on-two.

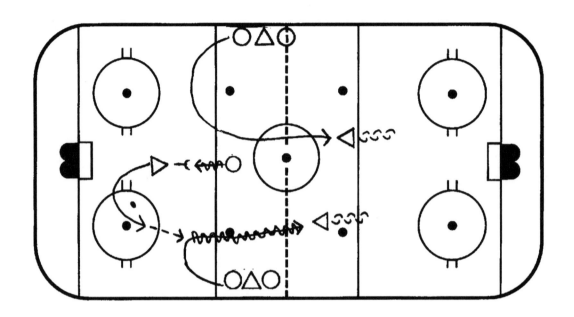

# Triples

A one-on-one, two-on-two, three-on-three continuous drill. The drill starts with a one-on-one. As the one-on-one is played out, two supporting forwards enter the zone. Upon gaining puck control, the supporting forwards rush up the ice to play two-on-two against two waiting defensemen.

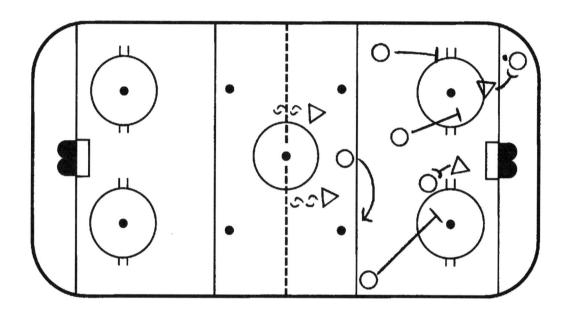

# Triples (continued)

As the two-on-two is played out, three supporting forwards enter the zone. Upon gaining puck control, these three supporting forwards rush up the ice to play against two waiting defensemen and a waiting forward. The drill continues with the same sequence of attacks or the sequence is altered on the coach's command.

**Notes:**

# Chapter 8

## Organization of Practices

*"It is the efficiency of your practice sessions that will determine how quickly your objectives will be met."*

Planning practices should not be done at the last minute or without having yearly objectives in place. It is important as a coach that time has been spent looking at the needs of your players, and the level of play required to be competitive. The objectives for the season then provide a framework for planning individual practices.

Proper planning of practices allows for the maximum usage of ice time and space. Without this planning time on task is reduced. Time on task is the true time spent on the rehearsal of task objectives. Repetition is fundamental in the development of skills, physical or cognitive, and is directly related to time on task. This concept, as it is applied in practice planning, has a definite role on the rate of transference from practice to game performance. By establishing a framework which uses low organizational methods in each session, a good flow or pace to practice is achieved. This flow or pace increases time on task. The linking of time on task and specificity of training (Transfer Training) improves the quality of practice.

Applying the following guidelines will lead to a well-organized practice, which will result in better use of practice time.

# The Presession

1. **Post a copy of the practice plan** in the dressing room and brief it with the players. Outline any objectives or themes for the session and any new drills or variations.

2. **Brief your assistants** on practice so that drill setup may take place during explanations or drill fillers, such as the whistle lap. This way idle time is reduced and active time increased. Involving the assistant coaches in practice planning also provides a dimension of understanding of the practice objectives. Understanding practice objectives will enhance the instructional abilities of the assistant coaches and improve their coach to player rapport.

3. **Organize drill enhancers** such as pucks, pylons, chairs, extra nets, ropes, shooting targets for immediate access during the practice sessions.

# The Practice Session

1. **Use a common meeting place for practice.** The area near the teaching board is best since announcements and instruction often require the teaching board. This provides convenience and saves time.

2. **Name the drills** so that players can identify them quickly, allowing for a reduction in drill explanation and idle time.

3. **Utilize your assistant coaches.** Assign responsibility in areas of instruction that both the head coach and assistants are comfortable with. This allows for full time and space usage since the ratio of coach to athlete is reduced significantly. An example would be one of the coaching staff members providing instructional observation or correction to an athlete while others continue the drill. Activity for the group is maintained while instructional support is being provided as required.

# 4. **Include practice formations** such as:

## The Empty Corner...

is an organizational technique that saves time and thereby maintains the tempo of the drill. The empty corner method is effective whenever line drills are part of a practice plan. For example, the Horseshoe drill in which the shooter skates back into line after taking a shot on goal. Traditionally the drill will continue in this manner until the coach blows the whistle, signalling that a change of sides is in order. However, by instructing the athletes to move to the empty or opposite corner after taking the shot on goal no whistling down of the drill is required. It is then easy for the coach to observe and keep track of the repetitions completed by his athletes. As well, the possibility for increasing the number of repetitions in a comparatively similar amount of time is evident. By having the athletes skate from alternating corners both sides of the body are being practiced equally. This is an obvious objective with regard to the athletes' development.

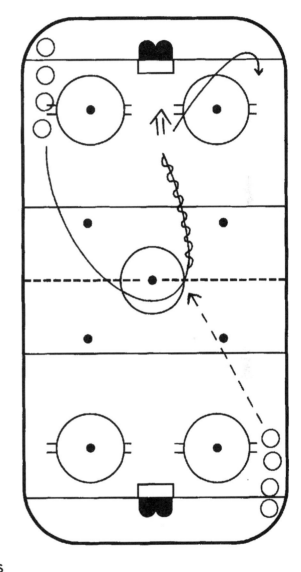

# The Whistle Lap...

is a technique that may be used to improve the pace and activity rate of practice. Upon completion of a drill the coach will blow the whistle and wave his stick in a circular fashion to signify the initiation and direction of the lap(s). The lap may be a straight out skate around or may take the form of backward skating, a combination of skating and puckhandling, or just about anything else the coach can come up with. A simple predetermined task is important since the objective is immediate movement and activity at a very high pace.

# Circuit Training . . .

improves the quality of practices by enabling a large volume of work and rehearsal to be achieved within a short frame of time. Concurrently the coach/player contact is improved, allowing for an increase in teaching, motivating, and support time. For example, a four-station circuit of two minutes per station and five players per station. Stations such as passing, shooting, skating agility, and puck control might be used. By running through the circuit once or twice, a high level of intensity and repetition is achieved. Idle time is also reduced.

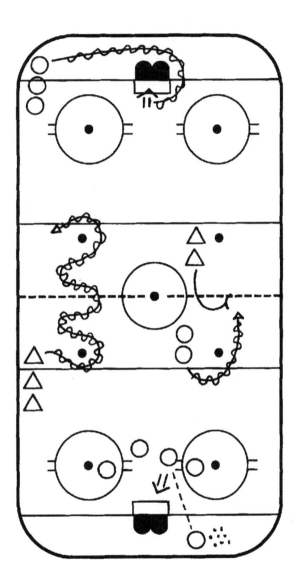

# The Four Blues . . .

is a formation used in practice that enables the coach to run a series of drills without losing valuable time to player relocation. The four blues formation is set up in neutral ice with the players divided into an equal number of forwards and defensemen, with pucks, at each "corner" of the formation. The "corners" are the spots where the blueline meets the boards. From this formation, individual skill drills, small group tactical, and conditioning drills can be executed with a high rate of repetition, thereby creating "flow" in the training session. Drills such as the single player Give-and-Go, to Linking drills provide the coach with an opportunity to maximize ice time and provide variety to training sessions.

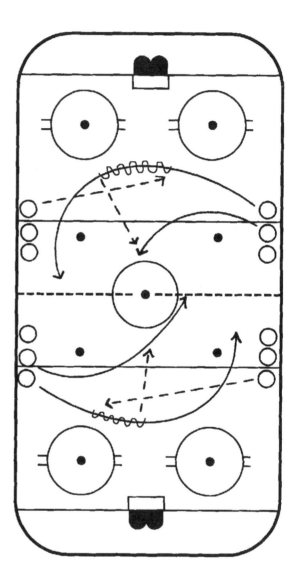

# The Assembly Line . . .

is a practice formation that enables the coach to incorporate variation and repetition within a single drill. Pucks are placed at strategic areas on the ice (usually the corners), so that the drill is repeatedly initiated by the player just completing the designated task. For example, players are lined up along the boards at neutral ice. On command, a player rushes toward the net completing a series of stickhandling maneuvers and shooting on goal. After finishing the play on goal the player swings toward the corner, "picks up" a puck, and makes a long diagonal pass to the next player in line. He then reenters the line or stops at the far side to establish a new line. The flow of the drill is uninterrupted, allowing the coaching staff to be available for player instruction.

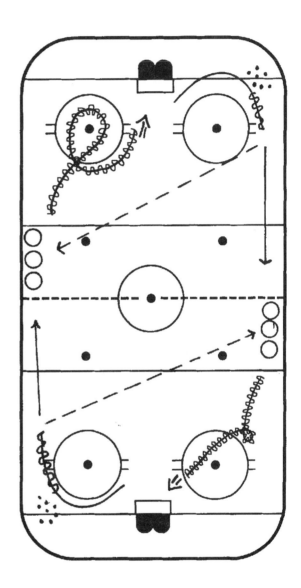

# The Postsession

Date and evaluate your practice sessions for future reference. By doing this a resource is developed for future use and comparisons.

*Preparation will improve practice efficiency.*

# Sample Practice On-Ice (1)

| | |
|---|---|
| Length | • 60 minutes |
| Objectives | • Skill rehearsal, tactics, and conditioning |
| Phase | • Precompetitive |
| Coaching staff | • The head coach and two assistants |
| Team size | • 20 players – 18 skaters and 2 goalies |
| Age group | • Bantam or Midget (14-15 or 16-17 year olds) |

| | | |
|---|---|---|
| 5 minutes | 1-on-0 Give-and-Go | – shoot to warm up goalies |
| 5 minutes | 2-on-0 Give-and-Go | – pass receiver drives net |
| 5 minutes | 2-on-1 Give-and-Go | – maintain flow |
| 5 minutes | 2-on-2 Link | – both ends at same time |

(Use 4 Blues Formation, page 88, for above)

| | |
|---|---|
| *1 minute* | **Water break** |

10 minutes     2-on-1 Transition drill

15 minutes     Specialized scrimmages
One zone, Ping Pong – 45 second shifts with 2 shift rests (work/rest ratio of 1:2).

*1 minute*     **Water break**

3 minutes     Laps
On whistle, change direction. Accelerate on change of direction for 20 feet (6 meters) then skate at three-quarter speed. Whistle sounds every 20 seconds (work/rest ratio of 1:1). Players carry a puck.

5 minutes     Cool down. Player time used for stretching or rehearsing individual skills at low-intensity level. Coaches float to help setup or assist in individual skill rehearsal.

# Sample Practice On-Ice (2)

| | |
|---|---|
| Length | • 60 minutes |
| Objectives | • Skill rehearsal, tactics, and conditioning |
| Phase | • Precompetitive |
| Coaching staff | • The head coach and two assistants |
| Team size | • 17 players – 15 skaters and 2 goalies |
| Age group | • Atom or Pee Wee (10-11 or 12-13 year olds) |

| | |
|---|---|
| 3 minutes | Mass Drill – each player has a puck and stickhandles through traffic while staying within the neutral ice zone. Goaltenders go through warmup drills with assistant coaches. |
| 10 minutes | Assembly line – Players line up along the boards at neutral ice with each line facing its own net. |

1. Skate the pylons, shoot, pick up, and pass to next player in line. Skate to next line.

2. Two players attack the goal. Upon completing the play at net, they initiate a breakout. One player picks up and passes the puck to the second player, waiting along the boards. The second player skates up and makes a diagonal pass to the next players in line. The original players then skate into line.

| | |
|---|---|
| *1 minute* | **Water break** |

| | |
|---|---|
| 15 minutes | Circuit (3 stations – 5 minutes per station) |

1. stickhandling drill (using preferred and nonpreferred hands), finish with shot on goal.

2. skating drills in neutral zone.

3. shooting drill (using preferred and nonpreferred hands), finish with shot on goal.

| | |
|---|---|
| *1 minute* | **Water break** |

| | |
|---|---|
| 15 minutes | Specialized scrimmages |

3-on-3 Outlet scrimmage and
3-on-3 Opposite Hands scrimmage

| | |
|---|---|
| 10 minutes | Tactical rushes |

1-on-1 Link      2-on-1 Link

2-on-2 Link

| | |
|---|---|
| 2 minutes | Cool down |

# SECTION FOUR

## Off-Ice Transfer Training

*Including skill development in a conditioning program
is both beneficial and fun.*

# Chapter 9

## Transfer Training

*"The objective is the immediate transference of the benefits of the muscular exercises toward the skill or skills being practiced."*

As a teenaged hockey player preparing for Junior camps, I always wanted to be as ready as possible for the upcoming season. While my brother lifted heavy weights, I incorporated hockey movements within my training. Shooting pucks off a small board, simulating hockey strides, and sprinting were tasks that reflected my desire to improve as a player. The first summer I set up the program I found myself in great shape and a step ahead of my own expectations. While I had no real idea as to how to train for hockey, the results were very gratifying.

The power components of my training were consistent in terms of preparing for the game of hockey. Hockey is a power game and, as such, training for power development only makes sense. This is not to say that strength training is not important. Strength training has its place within the yearly plan. However, in dealing with power conversion and optimal time use Transfer Training is equally important within a training plan.

The other obvious aspect of my training was the implementation of skill drills within my program. I shot puck after puck, and by summer's end my shooting skills had improved. Why not incorporate skill training within a physical training program?

Physical development benefits the athlete by improving endurance, agility, speed, flexibility, strength, and power. Athletes also train to reduce injuries and to improve recovery rates. However, **to compete, a standard level of skill is required for each level of play.** To ignore skill development during the off season (off the ice) is opportunity lost. To improve at the game you have to practice the game. Improving your strength and power plays a significant role in improving your play. But the techniques of performing the skills themselves are learned and reinforced only by the actual performance and practicing of those skills.

Dryland Transfer Training combines the actual performance of sport-specific skills with resistance training. It is continuous training that uses a circuit-style format. The participant will move from resistance-training exercises to skill-specific drills like puck shooting, and back again. The objective is the immediate transference of the benefits of the muscular exercises toward the skill or skills being practiced. For example, a set of bench presses is followed by a set of puck shooting, that is in turn followed by a set of plyometric leg exercises, and so on. While training, any planned recovery stations or periods are areas of active rest (low-intensity activity). In this way the heart rate is gradually lowered so that the athlete may continue with the circuit.

Circuit training is a complete form of training. The variation of resistance within the circuit trains the anaerobic capabilities of the muscular system, as well as the muscular components of strength. The overall volume and variance of intensity within the workouts train the cardiovascular system. Specificity and athleticism are addressed by the nature of the selected drills for each workout.

Skill development during the off season is a facet of training that is not emphasized with training programs available today. Yet, by practicing stick skills such as shooting and stickhandling, these skills can be heightened to new levels by utilizing time within training programs. As such, a more comprehensive and complete form of training – **Transfer Training** – is being undertaken by the athlete. The result is players with not only improved physical fitness, but with improved game-related skills.

A much desired objective for any athlete.

There is also a place for cognitive development within training. Research has shown that the inclusion of mental imagery into a physical training program accelerates and enhances the results of training, and with it its transference to performance.

For example, setting up a shooting station within an off-ice circuit session. The player is shooting pucks off a short board toward a target 20 feet (6 meters) away. A quick release and accuracy are the objectives. The player visualizes receiving a pass while "entering" the slot area. Upon "receiving" the pass, a quick shot is physically taken. This combination of mental rehearsal and physical training is explained in many books on mental training and I do encourage coaches to take the time to review the material available.

*"Visualization accelerates and enhances results."*

# Chapter 10

## Growth and Development

*"Objectives must correspond with the age phase the athlete is currently in, otherwise problems will occur."*

Training objectives within conditioning programs are of primary importance. However, those objectives must also correspond with the age phase the athlete is currently in, otherwise problems will occur. Having a resistance (weight-lifting) program coupled with skill drills is appropriate for Midget players (16-17 year olds), for example. But this program is not what a coach would apply with players who have not progressed far enough, physiologically speaking, such as Pee Wee players (12-13 year olds). Yet, by maintaining the skill drills and altering the resistance program from weights to body weight or agility activities, such as obstacle courses for example, you have customized the training program to better suit the age level you are working with.

Having a training program for Atoms (10-11 year olds) may seem extreme for coaches. However, the idea of shooting pucks at home and being involved in a wide array of activities such as soccer, bike riding, and touch football during the summer weeks will improve the fitness and skill levels of those Atom players. We might not think of calling this a training program, but for this age level it is the most appropriate "program". It is worthwhile to support this notion since it does encourage the physical, mental, social, and emotional benefits attributed to play during this phase of growth and development.

No matter what the age, it is important to have an element of fun associated with the purpose of training. Whenever the actual skills of the game, such as shooting, are part of a conditioning program, motivation to participate is higher. If the athlete enjoys the workouts, more time and effort will be put toward it. Enthusiasm toward workouts has obvious benefits.

# Chapter 11

## General Principles of Training

*"Principles provide a foundation for progressive training."*

PRINCIPLES
PRINCIPLES
PRINCIPLES
PRINCIPLES

To be effective, and to achieve the desired results, an understanding of the general principles and the methods used in training is required. These principles apply to both on- and off-ice workouts and provide a framework for progressive training. Without incorporating these principles into a program, the results will be sporadic at best, no matter what the method, and possibly even detrimental to anticipated objectives. By understanding these principles you will be able to "see" the direction of Transfer Training, and perhaps modify the program to better suit your athletes.

## 1. Specificity and Athleticsm

Just as the concepts of specificity and athleticsm can be used to make on-ice practices more efficient and transferable to game play, they also have an essential but overlooked role in off-ice training. Sport specificity is a factor in improving a player's skill and conceptual abilities. As mentioned in Chapter 3, it is specificity in training that allows for the replication of a desired skill and the rehearsal of the decision-making process needed during actual competition.

Puck shooting in the back yard is a common occurrence with most young athletes looking to improve their shot. The repetition involved in shooting puck after puck improves the skill and is directly transferable. The exercise is specific to the sport skill being trained. It is worth repeating that the more specific or closely related a movement is to the actual movement desired, the greater the rate of transference. This means that shooting pucks and stickhandling pucks will be important aspects to an off-ice program, because it maintains or improves the player's skills. This is a purpose of training.

Achieving the grace or smoothness of movement that are the traits of world-class players is one of the primary objectives of anyone who trains. Athleticsm is the driving force toward efficient movement. As mentioned in Chapter 3, the rate of learning is quicker, and the response time shorter, for well-coordinated athletes, as compared to those of a lower level of coordination. The inclusion of a variety of activities, such as skipping rope, tumbling, or game-type activities like basketball and golf, will lead to improved coordination. The principle of athleticism is often ignored when designing training programs. Its inclusion results in accelerating the rate of attaining all training objectives.

# 2. Periodization

Periodization is the planning of an athlete's year. This annual plan has three main phases; the Transition Phase, the Preparatory Phase, and the Competitive Phase. The **Transition Phase** is the period of time immediately after the competitive season. During this phase the athlete engages in recreational activities only. It is a period of relaxation and recovery that includes activities such as golf, casual bike rides, and any other activity of a recreational intensity.

The **Preparatory Phase** is the training phase. Resistance training and cardiovascular conditioning are used to prepare the athlete for the upcoming season. It is during this phase that intensity increases to training levels. Strength, power, and cardiovascular programs need to be properly planned for this phase so as to achieve optimal benefits from each. Improper or no planning at all can either diminish achievable training gains, or lead to **overtraining**. Overtraining occurs when intense training continues for too long a duration without sufficient recovery time. This may cause training progress to be slowed or even regress (Harre, 1986).

The **Competitive Phase** is the phase beginning with training camp and continuing into actual competition. During this phase technical and tactical skills are worked on.

Flexibility in planning during this phase of the yearly plan is important. The unpredictability of the competitive phase does not allow for coaches to blindly proceed with previously drawn up plans if those objectives are not being met. Adjustments in planning will more than likely be required. The recognition of failing objectives and the ability to correct during the coach's yearly plan is important. Often sessions are drawn up at the last minute or with little thought as to what the short-term or even long-term objectives of a program might be. The result is a loss of quality in training time and missed opportunities to build toward team and individual objectives.

One of those objectives is maintenance. After intense training during the preparation phase, training goals have been reached. Maintenance allows the athlete to retain those training gains, otherwise **detraining** will occur. The effects of detraining become apparent shortly after training ceases (Fleck, 1994). Detraining refers to the loss of any gains made by the athlete during his training period, if training were to cease. Strength training should be included once a week to maintain any previous gains.

With regards to the cardiovascular system research (Wilson & Hedberg, 1976) has indicated that the aerobic system will not be enhanced through game play itself, and it is not practical to utilize valuable ice time to aerobically train your athletes. The aerobic system and muscular strength must be maintained through off-ice sessions.

The utilization of Transfer Training as a maintenance program for the cardiovascular system, and for power conversion of the muscular system, will serve to maintain any gains the athlete attained during the Preparatory Phase. Such programs are easy to apply and modify to any type of schedule a team may be forced to endure throughout the course of a season.

During each of these phases the appropriate form(s) of training and conditioning are implemented with the final objective being improved performance during competition.

## *A yearly plan for training might look like the following;*

### Midget Hockey Training Cycle (16-17 year olds)

| Phase | Month | Activity |
|---|---|---|
| Transition | • April/May | • Recreational activities |
| General Preparatory | • May/July | • Strength training |
| Specific Preparatory | • July/August | • Transfer Training (Power) Technical training |
| Pre-Competitive | • September | • Transfer Training (Power) Technical training Tactical training |
| Competitive | • October/ March | • Transfer Training (Power) Technical training Tactical training |

# 3. Variety

Variation is one of the key principles of training. It promotes athleticism and maintains the athlete's interest. Variation in workload, intensity level, speed of movement, resistance, the type of muscle contraction, and the type of exercise or drill performed will all play a role in achieving training gains.

Programs such as circuit training allow for the principle of variation to be easily incorporated. Moving from one type of exercise (plyometric) to another type of exercise (ballestic) within the circuit exemplifies the ability to promote variety within training.

Modifying exercises by using various types of equipment (weights vs. medicine balls; skipping ropes vs. weighted skipping ropes) will also enhance training. Modifying movement patterns to be hockey specific in nature increases specificity in training. By moving a dumbbell in a wristshot or slapshot motion, a positive transfer from training to playing hockey has been achieved.

Variation leads to greater results in an off-ice training program and ultimately to an athletically stronger player.

# 4. Intensity

The athlete who approaches conditioning with no thought as to what objectives are desired, will not see the same degree of progress as the athlete who works through a training program intent on meeting or even surpassing the desired outcome. In other words, **"What you put in is what you get out."**

The intent to move a barbell with speed, to run the fastest distance, to bench press an additional 25 pounds is one of the driving forces in training gains. The athlete that trains with intent surpasses the one that doesn't because intent leads to intensity – the degree of effort put into an activity.

It is important, as a coach, to realize that intensity cannot and should not be maintained at the same level at all times. Appropriate intensity levels must be targeted for the appropriate phases of the training cycle, otherwise desired objectives will not be met, and may even be detrimental to the training. After the conclusion of a long hockey season, the intensity level should be low. However, intensity should be increasing continually as the player approaches training camp. Varying intensity will accelerate improvements in the athlete's physical and mental preparation. Without this variation, overtraining may result.

# 5. Volume

Volume refers to how often and how long an athlete trains. The volume decided upon will determine what aspects of the athlete's energy and muscular systems are trained. If, as a coach, you determine that a player needs to work on strength endurance, a program might be set up that involves training five times a week, using 3 sets of 20 repetitions per exercise with a light resistance. If a player needs to improve power, then the frequency could be three sessions per week with moderate weights and 4 sets of 8 repetitions.

As a coach it is also important to understand what volume of training you want your players to be involved in, according to the yearly plan. While in the Transition Phase, athletes should be engaged in low volume activities of a recreational nature. During the Preparatory Phase a much higher volume of work would be performed. Once the Competitive Phase begins it is important to know when to increase training volume and when to lower it. During the Competitive Phase training volume will reflect the competitive schedule. Training camps typically reflect a higher volume of on- and off-ice work since the competitive schedule has not yet begun. The volume of training during the competitive schedule is determined by days available. A three- or four-day break between games would allow training volume to increase to provide for a maintenance effect with regard to off-ice strength training and to maintain and work toward enhancing anaerobic capabilities on and off the ice. Volume increases in training during the Competitive Phase must be measured off with the athlete's recovery capabilities, otherwise overtraining will occur and hamper competitive performances.

# 6. Recovery

The concept of recovery has received increased attention during the last few years, with the primary drive coming from Europe. Different recovery methods have been experimented with and utilized in an effort to maximize future performances. Recovery can take the form of rest periods during the specified activity; rest periods directly after the specified sessions; and rest periods between subsequent sessions. By improving the quality of recovery an athlete is able to apply greater quality and volume to training schedules, and thereby accelerate gains. Improving recovery capabilities also allows the athlete to perform at a high level of intensity over a longer period of time, both during the length of the season and the competition itself. Planned recovery techniques will not only improve the athlete's ability to endure greater training loads but will also assist in reducing the risk of injury.

Recovery during training sessions may incorporate low-intensity activity. This activity, called **active recovery or active rest,** may be the same activity performed during training or an activity of a different nature. Active recovery should allow body functions to move toward a normal state, with minimal stress on the areas being trained (Harre, 1986). The inclusion of active recovery periods within practice sessions is critical. Low-intensity recovery periods allow the athlete to maintain quality within training sessions. Further to this, active recovery allows the athlete to refocus and optimize learning. Maximizing learning and the transference of learning equals quality in training.

Improving recovery times after training or competing is achieved by using various techniques, with the idea of avoiding adaptation. As the body adapts, the particular recovery technique used loses its effectiveness (Yessis, 1986). By varying the techniques targeted for improving recovery, such as cold showers, saunas, massage, and reflexology, adaptation is avoided. Stationary bike programs, that reflect the amount of playing time each player had that night, may also be used with the idea of removing lactic acid from the system so that recovery is quicker than usual.

On "off days", active recovery may be designed as a session itself. These "off days" can be used for fun and relaxation. Using low-intensity games, related or unrelated to hockey, gives the athlete an important mental and physical break.

By incorporating planned recovery activities, whether it be during a session, immediately following a session, or between sessions, your players will achieve better training results, and game performance will be improved.

# Chapter 12

## General Methods of Training

*" Methods are the framework for progressive training."*

The following methods of training are described here with the rationale that they are the primary methods associated with Transfer Training. Though the descriptions are brief they will provide information on the main concepts behind each method. Grasping the main concepts of each method will allow the coach to plan toward the objectives of a complete Transfer Training workout.

## 1. Weight Training (Power)

Due to the combative nature and speed in the game of hockey, power is required. The explosiveness of movement, associated with power, will play a greater role in hockey than maximum strength, due to the ever-changing nature of the game. Maximum strength and its development is the foundation for improving power, however, and as such holds a place in the athlete's training season.

Training will need to develop the components of power specifically toward the requirements of hockey. Training with light resistance exercises will assist in increasing power during the performance of sport-specific movements. The athlete is capable, under light resistance, of initiating a higher volume of repetitive and rapid movements without interfering with the coordination or form desired for successfully mimicking the specified skill. The use of skate weights, stick weights, parachutes, and weighted vests, for example, enable the athlete to perform under resistance while maintaining form. This important feature of light resistance training looks to improve power and, concurrently, the skill itself. Thus light resistance training allows for specificity in training.

When weight training, athleticism also comes into play with the utilization of heavy-resistance training, particularly the Olympic lifts. Split Cleans or the Clean and Jerk are weight training movements that develop coordination and power. As such, there is a positive transference toward athleticism. This athleticism in turn transfers positively in regard to performance. These Olympic lifts involve the large muscle groups of the body and are very demanding in the work load placed upon the training athlete. Olympic movements require proper technique and form to be beneficial, otherwise serious injury may easily occur. It is advisable for the novice athlete to prepare himself by training with light loads, until the proper form and techniques are mastered, before encompassing maximum lifts with Olympic movements.

During the course of weight training, combining the intent for explosiveness with an slow return phase will benefit the athlete, not only in his development of power, but also in maintaining the results over a longer period of time. The **intention of explosive movement** is the determining factor toward power development (Young, 1993). With the intention or effort to move quickly, the muscle becomes "spring loaded" in preparation for the series of contractions it is to be recruited for. This will increase the duration of tension within muscle fibers and the speed of muscle contraction. So, in the development and training of power, the intention of explosive movement is the crucial factor.

# 2. Ballistic Training

Ballistic training is a form of power training that addresses the problem of deceleration. When weight training, the movement of resistance is actually incomplete in terms of acceleration through the complete range of the movement. The bench press is an example. The barbell is actually slowed down significantly at the top of the press in order for the athlete to maintain control. (Newton & Kramer, 1994). Performing the movement completely without decelerating would require the barbell to leave the lifter's hands, at least momentarily.

Exercises such as the bench press, where the barbell leaves the hands, or jump squats are a form of ballistic speed training which, though effective, do carry a high percentage of risk for injury. In light of this, medicine ball workouts are a safer form of ballistic training that "carry" a quality of athleticism during performance. Younger players who are not physically ready for weight training or older athletes looking to supplement their training programs, can be put through a rigorous session of medicine ball drills that provide for progression in the desired physical attributes.

# 3. Plyometrics

A basic understanding of plyometrics is required when designing or implementing them within your program. Plyometrics, a form of speed strength or power training, involves the stretch-shortening cycle preceded by rapid prestretching. If you consider the traditional standing long jump, and add either a short quick hop prior to take off; or upon landing, immediately repeat the jump, it has become plyometric. **To be truly plyometric an exercise must carry three important components; there must be prestretching, a maximum effort, and minimal ground contact time.**

Plyometric exercises are categorized from low to high impact, such as skipping rope to drop jumps from elevations of greater than 15 inches (35 centimeters). Plyometrics can be designed for sport specificity by mimicking desired movements such as skating strides, and thereby allowing for improved power in the desired movement. Combining weight training with plyometrics, such as leg squats with short-distance striding, the athlete develops the qualities of power and, to an extent, strength endurance while also incorporating sport-specific movements for hockey. It is important to realize that plyometrics within a weight-training program is very demanding. Like any training program, a plyometrics program should be designed within the athlete's capabilities and experience.

# 4. Flexibility

The utilization of a flexibility program is important in the training and conditioning of the human body. This importance is not only relevant when the athlete undergoes resistance training, but flexibility also plays a role in speed and skill performance. Full range of movement is a direct factor in improving speed and coordination, since limited movement range detracts from the athlete's potential to learn and acquire skills. The athlete who has poor flexibility in the hipjoint area, for example, will not be able to fully utilize his legs in the skating motion, and will lose sought-after speed and maneuvering ability.

Flexibility programs are used as warmup, recovery, and cooldown sessions, and are directly related to the improvement of the range of motion of body segments. In addition, flexibility is associated with a reduction in activity-related injuries and the strengthening of tendons and ligaments. A properly conducted flexibility program assures the athlete of a full range of motion.

Stretching under slow and controlled movement is a safe and efficient method of flexibility training. Static and 3S (scientific stretching for sport) stretching are two such examples. The slow and deliberate movement of static stretching provides a measure of control and safety when compared to dynamic (bouncing) styles of stretching.

The 3S method (Holt, 197?) involves slow movements combined with an isometric contraction of the area being stretched. These contractions occur at three points in the range of the stretch being performed: at the introduction of the stretching movement, halfway through the segment's range of movement, and at the peak of the stretching movement.

An example is the sitting toe reach. Here the athlete sits with legs together, flat on the floor. The initial movement is to reach slightly forward and then try to return, against resistance from a partner, to an upright position. The contraction against resistance is maintained for 6 seconds. This is repeated, at the 50 percent range and 100 percent range of the stretch with a 6-second return phase against resistance for each level of stretch.

By using 3S contractions the athlete may stimulate the area being stretched and lead to enhanced flexibility over a shorter period of time.

# Chapter 13

## The Program

After having read through the principles and methods of training it is now time to outline the program of Transfer Training.

| April | May | June | July | August |
|---|---|---|---|---|
| Transition | Strength | Power (Transfer Training) | Strength | Power (Transfer Training) |

Transfer Training is done for three to six weeks during the Preparatory Phase of the yearly planning schedule. This may be broken up into two three-week sessions, with each session following a strength-training session of four weeks. Set up a training plan according to the time the athletes have available. The Transfer Training program is done four or five days a week at a minimum of 30 minutes per session.

On the days where there is no Transfer Training planned (off days) the athlete should be involved in other activities such as cycling, golf, or tennis. Any activity that enhances the athletic qualities is suitable.

| Mon. | Tues. | Wed. | Thurs. | Fri. | Sat. | Sun. |
|---|---|---|---|---|---|---|
| Transfer Training | | | Transfer Training | | | |

When using weights, movement is to be a combination of fast and slow. Each set will have movement that is to start with fast repetitions, include slow repetitions, and conclude with fast repetitions.

Between sets active recovery is utilized. This active recovery is anything from shooting pucks to shadow boxing. Active recovery maintains a level of intensity throughout the course of the workout. This maintaining of a manageable intensity level improves aerobic capacity which is directly related to endurance. As the aerobic capacity improves, the ability to do work at higher intensity levels also improves. In other words, endurance improves.

# Transfer Training Programs

This section includes sample programs for dryland Transfer Training. As you become more familiar with the techniques and premise of Transfer Training you will be able to modify the programs to reflect your objectives.

These programs are used during the Preparatory and Competitive phases.

## Sample Program (1)

### A BODY WEIGHT PROGRAM:

- Do 2 to 4 sets of 4 to 10 repetitions with movement as fast as possible.
- Complete the targeted number of sets in one group of exercises before moving on to the next group.

## Workload measurements

| Workload | Repetitions | Distance | Time (minutes) |
|---|---|---|---|
| Lower body | 40 | 280 yds.(260 m) | 10 |
| Upper body | 120 | | 1 |
| Skills | 100 (est.) | | 3½ |

### WARM-UP

- Light stretching and jogging on the spot       5 minutes

**SKIP**       3 minutes

### Stickhandle – Figure 8                      30 seconds

- ⬭ Use preferred and nonpreferred hands

### Ricochet Pushups                            8 repetitions

- ⬭ Feet placed upon chair or bench, back straight. Place an obstacle such as a water bottle between hands. Objective is to drive hands, from side to side, over the obstacle.

### Double hop verticals                        8 repetitions

- ⬭ Short bounce followed by a maximum-height vertical jump.

### SKIP                                        1 minute

## GROUP TWO:

### Shooting – specified targets

1 minute

- Use preferred and nonpreferred hands

### Hammer-throw

8 repetitions

- With both hands on the weight, twist torso from side to side, moving weight in hammer-throw fashion. At the peak of twist immediately change direction. Weight remains suspended directly in front of torso.

### Lateral leg jumps

8 repetitions

- Jumping side to side.

### SKIP

1 minute

## GROUP THREE:

**Clapping pushups**                              8 repetitions

**Standing long jump**                            4 repetitions
**& sprint burst – 15 yds. (14 m)**

**SKIP**                                          1 minute

### Passing – Over obstacles

1 minute

- Use preferred and nonpreferred hands

### Sprinter Skips – 25 yds. (23 m)

4 repetitions

- Take off on left leg while driving right knee up toward the chest. Upon ground contact with left leg repeat sequence for right leg. Maximize both vertical and horizontal distance while skipping predetermined distance.

### Heavy bag boxing

1 minute

### SKIP

1 minute

**Opposite Hand Stickhandle – Figure 8**    1 minute

**Double hop verticals**    8 repetitions
    **& sprint burst – 15 yds. (14 m)**

**Feet flat situps**    8 repetitions

**SKIP**    1 minute

**COOL DOWN**    5 minutes
    Light stretching

# Sample Program (2)

In this next sample, circuit time per station varies according to the individual's objectives for each session. The technical stations are rehearsed at as high a speed as possible, however, control is essential to mastering each skill. Since the skill stations will not be as taxing, they take the role of active recovery. The overall duration of activity will tax the cardiovascular system. The circuit duration can be varied to suit individual needs.

## Workload measurements

| Workload | Repetitions | Distance | Time (minutes) |
|----------|-------------|----------|----------------|
| Full body | 24 | | 9 or 18 |
| Upper body | 48 | | |
| Lower body | 24 | | |
| Skills | will vary | | 7½ |

## MOVE FROM STATIONS 1-2-3-2-1-2 . . .

- Station 1 do 1 or 2 minutes per exercise.

- Station 2 is an active rest station. Do 30 seconds of intense repetitions to complete the set for each skill.

- Station 3 uses a weight or load of 30-50% of one repetition maximum. Do 8 repetitions per exercise. Upon completing a set from Station 3, move to Station 2 as active rest.

- Program is complete when Stations 1 and 3 have been repeated three times.

## WARM-UP

- Light stretching and jogging on the spot     5 minutes

## STATION 1.  POWER WORK

### Box heavy bag

### Skip

### Vertical kicks

- Jump and kick as high as you can.

### Shooting                                    30 seconds

-  Use preferred and nonpreferred hands

### Passing                                     30 seconds

- Use the saucer pass
- Use preferred and nonpreferred hands

### Stickhandling                               30 seconds

- Use preferred and nonpreferred hands

## STATION 3. WEIGHT TRAINING

**Bench Press**                                    8 repetitions

**Squats**                                          8 repetitions

**Military Press**                                  8 repetitions

**Wrist Curls**                                     8 repetitions

## COOL DOWN                                        5 minutes

&#128; Light stretching and jogging on the spot

# Sample Program (3)

By utilizing the concept of trisetting, an increased workload is attainable without hampering performance.

- Move from exercise to exercise within each grouping with minimal rest. Do rest however upon completing a set of three exercises.

- Do 2 sets of the number of repetitions indicated before moving onto the next grouping.

## Workload measurements

| Workload | Repetitions | Distance | Time (minutes) |
|---|---|---|---|
| Full body | | | |
| Upper body | 32 | | |
| Lower body | 16 | 130 yds. (120 m) | |
| Skills | will vary | | 5 |

**WARM-UP**

- Light stretching and jogging on the spot          5 minutes

**Sprinter skips – 25 yds. (23 m)**     2 repetitions

**Ricochet pushups**     8 repetitions

**Frog kicks**     8 repetitions

☞ A vertical jump bringing both legs up and attempting to touch the toes.

## Hammer-throw

8 repetitions.

## Long jump,
## 90° turn/sprint – 20 yds. (18.5 m)

2 repetitions

- Jump as far as possible, upon impact turn and sprint. The turn and sprint should be as quick as possible after impact from the long jump.

## Striding – 20 yds. (18.5 m)

2 repetitions

- Running with wide strides. Movement mimics skating stride.

## GROUP C

### 10 pucks of rapid fire

3-5 repetitions

- Target shooting – 20 ft. (6 m)

### 2 minutes of 10 seconds on 10 seconds off – stickhandling drills

2 repetitions

- Example: figure 8s

### 45 seconds of feet flat situps

2 repetitions

### COOL DOWN

5 minutes

- Light stretching and jogging on the spot

# Sample Program (4)

This is a superset program that builds endurance and power. A superset is a series of exercises that are performed with minimal rest between sets.

- The full program must be completed in 7½ minutes. If successful, the intensity (number of repetitions) or the resistance (weight) is increased.

- The program is 5 sets with 10 seconds of rest between each set

- For example, complete exercises 1 to 4, have a 10 second break, then continue with the second set. If able to complete all 5 sets within allocated time then add repetitions or resistance.

- Start with 8 repetitions per exercise and build to 10 repetitions. Sliding to one side and back again equals one repetition on the sliding board.

## WARM-UP

- Light stretching and jogging on the spot       5 minutes

## 1. Bench press

- Use weight of 30-50% of one repetition maximum

## 2. Medicine ball behind head toss (seated)

## 3. Medicine ball chest pass (seated)

## 4. Sliding board and stickhandling

## COOL DOWN                                   5 minutes

- Light stretching and jogging on the spot

# A Goalie Program

The following goalie specific drills can be used in place of the non-goalie skill drills for each of the previous program samples to create specific goalie programs.

1. **Reflex saves.** A partner directs tennis balls, with a tennis racquet, from behind the goalie toward a wall. The goalie must react to the incoming ball and make the appropriate save.

2. **Puck shooting.** Goalie practices puck shooting toward a target.

3. **Area saves.** Goalie practices technique as shots are directed at him from in front. Tennis racquet and tennis balls used.

# Summation

The fact that you have picked up this book and read it says that you are a committed coach. By trying these ideas and samples you will see the successful results that Transfer Training can bring to your team. As you become more familiar with the methods and techniques, I'm sure you will devise many of your own game-like drills.

Proper preparation leads to perfection. It's your preparation that will influence your practice sessions and overall yearly plans. Having clear objectives and an understanding of general principles of training is your framework. Your players will enjoy practices more, you'll see better results in your players' progress and, just as importantly, you as a coach will share in the excitement of learning and achievement.

# LOSSARY

**Active Rest** • low intensity activity during rest periods (e.g.) walking after a sprint.

**Aerobic** • "with oxygen" Continuous activity of a submaximal intensity allowing the muscles to derive energy from oxygen intake (e.g.) jogging.

**Anaerobic** • "without oxygen" Short bouts of maximal level intensity that require the muscles to derive energy from chemical changes without oxygen (e.g.) 50 yard or meter sprint.

**Athleticism** • the athletic qualities such as coordination and balance associated with movement in sport.

**Concentric** • muscular movement that shortens the muscle when contracting (e.g.) the upward motion of a bicep curl.

**Detraining** • loss of any gains, muscular or cardiovascular, as a result of a stoppage in training.

**Eccentric** • muscular movement that lengthens the muscle during contraction of that particular muscle (e.g.) the slow downward movement of a bicep curl.

**Isometric** • muscle contraction against an immovable object (e.g.) pushing against a wall.

**Specificity** • movements that simulate or mimic the actual sport related movement (e.g.) incorporating skating-like strides into running.

**Symmetrization** • training of non dominant side or limb (e.g.) a right handed player practicing shooting left handed.

**Transference** • action of transferring the qualities of learning (e.g.) shooting pucks in an off-ice setting to improve on-ice performance.

**Transfer Training** • method of training that emphasizes sport specific movements and replication of game-like situations.

# Bibliography

Arnett, M. "A Review of Concurrent Strength and Endurance Training". *SPORTS* Vol. 13, No. 2, 1993, 1-6.

Arnheim, D. D. & Arnheim, H. *Modern Principles of Athletic Training* (7th ed.). St. Louis, MO: Times, Mirror, and Mosby, 1989.

Bell, G. J., Petersen, S. R., Quinney, H. A., & Wenger, H. A., "Sequencing of Endurance and High-velocity Strength Training." *Canadian Journal of Sport Sciences,* Vol. 13, No. 4, 1988, 214-219.

Blatherwick, J. *Over-Speed Skill Training for Hockey.* Colorado Springs, CO: USA Hockey, 1992.

Bompa, T. O. *Power Training for Sport.* Ottawa, ON: Coaching Association of Canada, 1994.

Bompa, T. O. *Theory and Methodology of Training; The Key to Athletic Performance.* Dubuque, IO: Kendall/Hunt Publishing, 1990.

Boyle, M. "Explosive Power for Hockey." *Hockey Coaching Journal,* Vol. 4, No. 3, 1992, 11.

Burke, E. "The Wisdom of Cross Training." *Strength and Conditioning,* Vol. 16, No. 1, 1994, 58-60.

Canadian Amateur Hockey Association. *Proceedings of "Advanced II" Level Seminar.* Quebec City, QC, 1994.

Canadian Amateur Hockey Association. *Advanced Level Coaches Manual.* National Coaching Certification Program. Ottawa, ON, 1990.

Chu, D. A. *Jumping into Plyometrics.* Champaign, IL: Leisure Press, 1992.

Counsilman, J. E. "The Importance of Speed in Exercise." In E. J. Burke (Ed.), *Toward an Understanding of Human Performance: Readings in Exercise Physiology for the Coach and Athlete* (pp. 25-28). Ithaca, NY: Mouvement Publications, 1977.

Elson, P. "The Testing and Evaluation of the Hockey Player." In R. Lonetto & J. Marshall (Eds.), *Total Hockey* (pp. 256-302). Markham, ON: LR & Associates, 1997.

Fleck, S. "Detraining: Its Effects on Endurance and Strength." *Strength and Conditioning,* Vol. 16, No.1, 1994, 22-28.

Fox. E., Bowers, R., and Foss, M. *The Physiological Basis for Exercise and Sport* (5th Ed.). Dubuque, IO: Brown and Benchmark, 1993.

Harman, E. "Biomechanical Factors in Human Strength." *Strength and Conditioning,* Vol. 16, No. 1, 1994, 46-53.

Harman, E. "Strength and Power: A Definition of Terms." *National Strength and Conditioning Association Journal,* Vol. 15, No. 6, 1993, 18-20.

Harre, D. "Recovery: Part two: Overtraining." *SPORTS* , August, 1986, 1-4.

Holt, L. E. *Scientific Stretching for Sport.* Halifax, NS: Sport Research Limited, 197?

Jette, M. "The Physiological Basis of Conditioning Programs for Ice Hockey Players." In E. J. Burke (Ed.), *Toward an Understanding of Human Performance: Readings in Exercise Physiology for the Coach and Athlete* (pp. 68-72). Ithaca, NY: Mouvement Publications, 1977.

King, I. "Plyometric Training: In Perspective Part 1." *SPORTS*, Vol. 13, No. 5, 1993, 1-11.

King, I. "Plyometric Training: In Perspective Part 2." *SPORTS*, Vol. 13, No. 6, 1993, 1-11.

Koloskov, V. "Conditioning the Hockey Player." In F. Landry & W. A. R. Orban (Eds.), *Ice Hockey: International Symposium on Research and Development in Ice Hockey* (pp. 31-35). Miami, FL: Symposia Specialists, 1978.

La Chance, P. "Plyometric Exercise." *Strength and Conditioning*, Vol. 17, No. 4, 1995.

Lovering, K. *Personal Communication.* June, 1997.

MacAdam, D. and Reynolds, G. *Hockey Fitness: Year-Round Conditioning On and Off the Ice.* Champaigne, IL: Leisure Press, 1988.

MacDougall, J. D., Wenger, H. A. & Green, H. J. *Physiological Testing of the High Performance Athlete* (2nd ed.). Champaign, IL: Human Kinetics Books, 1991.

Masterson, G.L., and Brown, S.P. "Effects of Weighted Rope Jump Training on Power Performance Tests in Collegians." *Journal of Strength and Conditioning Research,* Vol. 7, No. 2, 1993, 108-114.

McFarlane, B. "Developing Maximum Running Speed." *SPORTS,* September, 1984, 1-7.

Newton, R. U. and Kraemer, W. J. "Developing Explosive Muscular Power: Implications for a Mixed Methods Training Strategy." *National Strength and Conditioning Association,* Vol. 16, No. 5, 1994, 20-31.

Poliquin, C. "Variety in Strength Training." *SPORTS* Vol. 8, No. 8, 1988, 1-7.

Reed, A., Ablack, D., and McNeely, E. "Alactic Strength Training." *SPORTS,* Vol. 12, No. 7, 1992, 1-5.

Rhodes, T. and Twist, P. *The Physiology of Ice Hockey : A Testing and Training Manual.* Vancouver, BC: University of British Columbia, 1990.

Sage, G. *Motor Learning and Control: A Neuropsychological Approach.* Dubuque, IO: William C. Brown, 1984.

Schmidtbleicher, D. "Strength Training: Part II: Structural Analysis of Motor Strength Qualities and its Application to Training." *SPORTS,* September, 1985, 1-10.

Scholich, M. *Circuit Training for All Sports.* Toronto, ON: Sports Books Publisher, 1992.

Siff, M. "Understanding the Mechanics of Muscle Contraction." *National Strength and Conditioning Association Journal,* Vol. 15, No. 5, 1993, 30-33.

Starosta, W. "Movement Symmetrization as a Method of Co-ordination Improvement in Children." In R. Malina (Ed.), *Young Athletes: Biological, Psychological, and Educational Perspectives* (pp. 67-283.) Champaign, IL: Human Kinetics, 1988.

Stone, M. H. "Roundtable: Aerobic Training in Power Sports". *National Strength and Conditioning Association Journal*, Vol. 6, No. 5, 1984, 10-19.

Tarasov, A. *Road to Olympus*. Toronto, ON: Griffin House, 1969.

Taylor, J. "Start With Your Lungs and Legs." *Sport Talk*, Vol. 8, No. 2, 1979, 1,3,6.

Taylor, T. *Lloyd Percival's Total Conditioning for Hockey*. Toronto, ON: Fitzhenry and Whiteside, 1978.

Toth, T. "Helping Young Players to Understand the Game On-ice." *Proceedings from International Hockey Coaches Seminar*, Calgary, Alberta, 1994.

Twist, P. and Rhodes, T. "The Bioenergetic and Physiological Demands of Ice Hockey." *National Strength and Conditioning Association Journal*, Vol. 15 No. 5, 1993, 68-70.

Wathen, D. "Rest Periods." In T. Baechle (Ed.), *Essentials of Strength Training and Conditioning*, (pp. 451-454). Champaign, IL: Human Kinetics, 1994.

Westerlund, E. *Personal Communication*. December, 1994.

Westerlund, E. *Transition: from Game to Practice*. Calgary, AB: Canadian Hockey Centre of Excellence, 1994.

Wilson, G. and Hedberg, A. *Physiology of Ice Hockey: A Report*. Ottawa, ON: Canadian Amateur Hockey Association, 1976.

Yessis, M. "Training for Power Sports, Part 1 and 2." *National Strength and Conditioning Association*, Vol. 17, No. 1, 1995, 68-73.

Yessis, M. *Secrets of Soviet Sports Fitness and Training*. New York, NY: Arbor House, 1987.

Yessis, M. "Recovery, Part 1." *SPORTS*, July, 1986, 1-6.

Young, W. "Training for Speed/Strength: Heavy vs Light Loads." *National Strength and Conditioning Association Journal*, Vol. 15, No. 5, 1993, 34-42.

# Symbols – Drill Legend

| | |
|---|---|
| - - - - - -> | Pass |
| ====> | Shot |
| ———( | Checking |
| ⌒⌒⌒⌒⌒ | Backward Skating |
| ———> | Direction of movement |
| ∿∿∿∿∿> | Direction of movement carrying a puck |
| ———⊣ | Support |
| ○ | Offensive Player |
| △ | Defensive Player |
| ⊗ | Extra Player |
| **c** | Coach |
| ⊙⊙ | Pucks |

# Share Perfect Practice

Order *Perfect Practice* at $19.95 per book (G.S.T. included) plus $4.00 (total order) for shipping and handling.

Number of copies _____ x $19.95 = $ _____

Shipping and handling _____ = $ _____4.00_____

Total enclosed _____ = $ _____

U.S. and international orders $19.95, payable in U.S. funds./ Price is subject to change.

NAME: _____

STREET: _____

CITY: _____ PROV./STATE _____

COUNTRY _____ POSTAL CODE/ZIP _____

Please make cheque or money order payable to:     **Centax Books & Distribution**
**1150 Eighth Avenue**
**Regina, Saskatchewan**
**Canada    S4R 1C9**

For fund raising or volume purchases, contact **Centax Books & Distribution** for volume rates.

Please allow 3-4 weeks for delivery

- - - - - - - - - - - - - - - - - - - ( • ) - - - - - - - - - - - - - - - - - - - -

# Share Perfect Practice

Order *Perfect Practice* at $19.95 per book (G.S.T. included) plus $4.00 (total order) for shipping and handling.

Number of copies _____ x $19.95 = $ _____

Shipping and handling _____ = $ _____4.00_____

Total enclosed _____ = $ _____

U.S. and international orders $19.95, payable in U.S. funds./ Price is subject to change.

NAME: _____

STREET: _____

CITY: _____ PROV./STATE _____

COUNTRY _____ POSTAL CODE/ZIP _____

Please make cheque or money order payable to:     **Centax Books & Distribution**
**1150 Eighth Avenue**
**Regina, Saskatchewan**
**Canada    S4R 1C9**

For fund raising or volume purchases, contact **Centax Books & Distribution** for volume rates.

Please allow 3-4 weeks for delivery

**PERFECT PRACTICE**